Issues in Psychology, Psychotherapy, and Judaism

Edited by
Seymour Hoffman

UNIVERSITY PRESS OF AMERICA,® INC.
Lanham • Boulder • New York • Toronto • Plymouth, UK

Copyright © 2007 by
University Press of America,® Inc.
4501 Forbes Boulevard
Suite 200
Lanham, Maryland 20706
UPA Acquisitions Department (301) 459-3366

Estover Road
Plymouth PL6 7PY
United Kingdom

All rights reserved
Printed in the United States of America
British Library Cataloging in Publication Information Available

Library of Congress Control Number: 2007921831
ISBN-13: 978-0-7618-3707-7 (paperback : alk. paper)
ISBN-10: 0-7618-3707-8 (paperback : alk. paper)

∞™ The paper used in this publication meets the minimum
requirements of American National Standard for Information
Sciences—Permanence of Paper for Printed Library Materials,
ANSI Z39.48—1984

The book is affectionately dedicated to the
Rothstein siblings and their spouses:
Louis, z"l and Ann Rothstein
Nathan, z"l and Ruth, z"l Rothstein
Irving, z"l and Gussie, z"l (Rothstein) Hoffman

Contents

Foreword		vii
Preface		ix
Acknowledgments		xiii

PART 1   PSYCHOLOGY AND JUDAISM

1	Increasing Clergy–Clinician Cooperation Through Education and Dialogue	1
2	Accidental Death: A New Look at an Ancient Model	7
3	Homosexuality: A Religious and Political Analysis	20
4	Rabbinic Insights into Behavior Change	28
5	Helpmates: Mother and Father as Cotherapy Model	31
6	Manipulation in Psychotherapy: Rabbinic View	35

PART 2   PSYCHOTHERAPY AND JUDAISM

7	The Care of the Ultra-orthodox Community	43
8	Initial Religious Counseling for a Male Orthodox Adolescent Homosexual	54
9	Rabbinic Interventions in Cases of Pathological Guilt	61
10	Psychotherapy and Honoring Parents	70
11	Halacha and Psychological Treatment Dilemmas and Conflicts	75

Foreword

The present volume focuses on the interface between psychology, psychotherapy and Judaism. The topics considered are varied and relate to theoretical as well as practical issues. Thus for example, in depth, original psychological insights and descriptions of certain religious laws and familiar biblical incidents are offered together with reports of effective therapeutic treatments involving rabbis and psychologists. Markedly differing opinions of various rabbinic authorities regarding psychotherapy, ranging from total rejection, to acceptance under certain limited conditions, to cooperation with therapists, are detailed. Rich clinical case material illustrating treatment issues that have relevance in terms of Jewish law, as well as treatment dilemmas arising from conflicts between Jewish law and aspects of psychotherapy as generally practiced, are also presented. Examples of psychological wisdom and insights of rabbis and religious leaders, ancient and contemporary, in effecting change in people, as well as guidelines on how to treat ultra-orthodox patients, are also clearly presented.

The wealth of information and the sensitive and significant issues discussed, lend importance to this book. Perhaps even more important is the very fact that appropriate attention is called to the significance of religious issues in psychotherapy with observant Jews, a subject that has until now received only scant consideration in the psychological literature. Moreover, the descriptions of positive outcomes of cooperation between mental health workers and rabbis in psychological treatment, point to direction for further work and development.

Rabbis, guidance counselors, therapists, mental health practitioners, as well as those interested in the interface between psychology, psychotherapy and Judaism, will find interest and benefit from reading this book.

Professor Lilly Dimitrovsky, Bar-Ilan University

Preface

Religion (Judaism) and mental health (psychology/psychotherapy) are two topics that continue to intrigue specialists and lay people alike. Each has been viewed in any number of lights, and ample controversy surrounds both areas of study. The same is true for the ways in which they are thought to relate to one another.

From the very beginning of the development of psychology as a discipline there has been a tense dialogue between psychology and religion because of the significant overlap in interests. Psychology aspires to understand the soul of man, psychotherapy to minister and cure his emotional ailments and conflicts and change him for the better. So does religion. However, their goals, values and means are frequently far apart and at odds with each other. Religion has in the past and continues in the present to view psychology as contradicting their foundations and values and even aspiring to replace it, while many mental health professionals view religion as a pathology which requires treatment.

On one extreme, there are leading mental health practitioners (psychologists and psychiatrists) who are known for their personal rejection of religious values and of constructing psychological theories that construed religion as primitive and pathological. Freud (1907) regarded religion as a "universal obsessional neurosis" while Ellis (1980) was of the opinion that, "The devoutly religious person tends to be inflexible, closed, intolerant and unchanging. Religiosity is in many respects equivalent to irrational thinking and emotional disturbance. The elegant therapeutic solution to emotional problems is to be quite unreligious".

However, there are a considerable amount of clinicians that take a well reasoned middle ground, maintaining that religion has the potential to be either positive or negative in its effects on mental health. They point out that religion can safeguard mental health by acting as a haven from life's difficulties and by providing structure meaning and purpose in life, or it can be a hazard by sponsoring the expression of psychological abnormality.

Extreme points of view and positions are also expressed and taken by religious leaders and spokesmen, generally from the ultra-orthodox camp, who view psychology/psychotherapy as a threat to Judaism and religious values, and whose pronouncements vary from temperate cautious criticism and advice to ridicule and venomous accusations and outright prohibition against seeking psychological help.

Amsel, (1969) a haredi mental health professional opined, "... all forms of "secular psychology", including psychoanalysis, behaviorism, ego psychology, etc., must in effect, be abandoned by the faithful "Torah psychologist". "All secular psychology is atheistic, denying Man his Free Choice".

Sosevsky, (2002) in a long and comprehensive paper, clearly delineates the conflict between Judaism and psychology/psychotherapy. She presents possible resolutions and classifies them into three models, the separation, integration and reconstruction models, which are briefly described and analyzed.

The separation model refers to therapists who live their lives according to religious values and work according to strictly professional values.

The integration model combines various approaches to synthesizing religion and psychology/psychotherapy by attempting to reframe psychological concepts, backing up psychological concepts and theories with Torah ideas and sources, and drawing parallels between various psychological schools of thought and religious movements.

The reconstruction model refers to new theories and approaches developed by therapists who reject the above models in favor of new theories which are inspired by Judaism.

In the last decade or so, there has been a general resurgence of investigative interest in the myriad of relationships between Judaism and psychology/psychotherapy which has enhanced our understanding of the complex interface between them. This book contains a collection of articles that discuss a wide spectrum of issues and topics concerning the interface between psychology, psychotherapy and Judaism, such as: a political and religious analysis of homosexuality; dilemmas and conflicts that face religious psychotherapists; a discussion of the problems and difficulties in treating religious patients and the ultra-orthodox community in particular; and examples of the successful collaboration of rabbis and psychologists in the treatment of psychiatric patients.

Hopefully, this book will provide food for thought and stimulate further discussion and exploration of issues and topics regarding the interface between psychology, psychotherapy and Judaism.

REFERENCES

A Amsel, *Judaism and psychology*. (New York: Feldheim, 1969).
A Ellis, "Psychotherapy and atheistic values: A response to A. E. Bergin's, "Psychotherapy and religious values." *J Consult Clin Psychol*, 48, (1980): 635–39.
S Freud, "Obsessive actions and religious practices, (1907)", Pp. 115–27 Vol. 9 in *Complete Psychological Works of Sigmund Freud*, edited and translated by J Strachey. London, England: Hogarth, 1959.
B Sosevsky, "Psychotherapy and Judaism: Conflicts and Resolutions." *ATID Online Journal*, (2002).

Recommended Readings:

MH Spero *Judaism and Psychology: Halakhic Perspectives*. (New York: Ktav Publishing/Yeshiva University Press, 1980).
D Greenberg and E Witztum, *Sanity and Sanctity: Mental Health Work Among the Ultra-Orthodox in Jerusalem*. (New Haven: Yale University Press, 2001).

Acknowledgments

The editor thanks the authors and publishers for their permission to reprint the respective articles, Drs. Shlomo and Miriam Sklarz and Betty Hoffman for their input and assistance, and to Dr. Richard and Mrs. Marcia (Rothstein) Kashnow for their generosity and support.

CREDITS

The editor gratefully acknowledges permission to reprint material from the following sources:

Chapters 1: Journal of Jewish Medical Ethics and Halacha, 4, 2, 2004. Schlesinger Institute.

Chapter 2: Bekhol Derakhekha Daehu, Journal of Torah Scholarship, 14, 2004. Copyright, Bar-Ilan University Press. Ramat-Gan, Israel.

Chapter 3: Tradition: A Journal of Orthodox Jewish Thought, 27, 3, 1993. Published by the Rabbinical Council of America. Copyright by the author.

Chapter 4: B'Or Ha'Torah, Journal of Science, Art and Modern Life in the Light of the Torah, 13, 2002. Published by Shamir.

Chapter 5: B'Or Ha'Torah, Journal of Science, Art and Modern Life in the Light of the Torah, 14E, 2004. Published by Shamir.

Chapter 7: Israel Journal of Psychiatry and Related Sciences, 28, 4, 1991. Gefen Publishing House Ltd., Jerusalem.

Chapter 8: Tradition: A Journal of Orthodox Jewish Thought, 29, 2, 1995. Published by the Rabbinical Council of America.

Chapter 10: Israel Journal of Psychiatry and Related Sciences, 4, 38, 2, 2001. Gefen Publishing House Ltd., Jerusalem.

Chapters 11: Journal of Jewish Medical Ethics and Halacha, 4, 2, 2004. Schlesinger Institute.

Part One

PSYCHOLOGY AND JUDAISM

Chapter One

Increasing Clergy-Clinician Cooperation Through Education and Dialogue

Seymour Hoffman, Ph.D., Nina Guy, M.D., Benny Feldman, Ph.D.

The attitude of orthodox rabbis toward mental health practitioners varies from outright hostility and distrust to respect and cooperation. Those identified with the ultra-orthodox camp generally view psychotherapists as a threat to religion and religious values, while modern orthodox rabbis generally relate to them as colleagues in ministering to the emotional and psychological needs of people in distress. The former group, generally, is highly vocal in its condemnation and criticism, while the latter group, generally, is rather subdued and guarded in its support of them.

Ultra-orthodox pronouncements vary from temperate, cautious criticism and advice, to ridicule and belittlement, to venomous accusations and outright prohibitions against seeking psycho-therapists' counsel.

"It is forbidden to go to a psychologist or psychiatrist who is a heretic or atheist . . . one must seek out a psychologist or psychiatrist who keeps the Torah. If this is not possible, then one can even go to a heretic or atheist, but it must be stipulated and he must promise not to discuss matters of belief and the Torah with the patient." (*Igrot Moshe, Yoreh De'ah*, 2:57).

"Even the best therapists have nothing to offer those whose sins have brought them to depression or sadness, for the help they need is from those knowledgeable in Torah, who are the real healers of souls . . . Psychologists and psychiatrists steal a lot of money from the patient and let him imagine that he will be healed." (*Tshuvot VeHanhagot*, 1:465, Rabbi Moses Sternbuch).

The haredi newspaper "*Yated Ne'eman*" reported on a halachic ruling by Rabbi Shmuel Auerbach, head of the *Ma'alot haTorah* Yeshiva in Jerusalem, that prohibited psychological counseling because "psychological treatment is the advice of the devil and the evil impulse and a terrible obstacle."

In the Jewish Tribune, an orthodox newspaper in England, Rabbi Shmuel Wosner, a recognized decisor from Bnei Brak, was quoted as stating, "their (psychologists) advice is the counsel of the wicked and it usually results in evil."

In his "Mishneh Halachot" (part 4, p. 127), Rabbi Menashe Hakatan (Klein) cites an article by Rabbi Moshe Deutch, head of the Katamon Religious court in London, entitled, "Turn not to soothsayers in the guise of psychologists", where the author makes several points: 1. Rabbi S. Z. Auerbach was of the opinion that "going to them (psychologists) results in much corruption"; 2. The Hazon Ish explicitly stated that one should not go to psychologists because they corrupt more than they repair; 3. The author of "Kehilat Yaacov" was of the same opinion.

In response to a question posed to him at a lecture he delivered at the Annual "Nefesh Israel" Conference (2004), Rabbi Yehoshua Neuwirth responded, "It is prohibited to refer patients to psychiatrists. Psychiatrists stupefy the soul."

At a conference held at Bar-Ilan University (March, 2005), entitled, "Professional Collaboration between Rabbis and Psychologists", in which rabbis and mental health practitioners participated, three prominent national religious rabbis presented their views on the above subject.

Rabbi Yisroel Meir Lau, former chief rabbi of Israel and presently chief rabbi of Tel-Aviv, pointed out that the relationship between rabbis and psychologists is in principle similar to that between halacha and medicine but stressed the difference between the objective physician and the subjective psychologist. "The psychologist", he said, "does not operate in a bubble, and something of his faith, his world view and values are also imprinted on his treatment methods."

Rabbi Shlomo Aviner, head of the Ateret Cohanim Yeshiva in Jerusalem, and rabbi of the settlement Bet El, opined that "halacha and psychology are two different worlds that can go together despite the fact that they speak two different languages", continuing the same line. "The psychologist deals with that that exists, whereas the rabbi deals with that that should exist."

Rabbi Yaacov Ariel, chief rabbi of Ramat Gan, put an even finer point on the matter. "The problem is that the psychologist suggests to the patient that he comes to terms with reality, whereas the rabbi suggests that he perfect the reality. If the psychologists continue to propose to the patients to come to terms with reality, the rabbis will continue to hesitate about referring people to them."

Isolated reactions in support of psychological treatment argue that, "Amateur dabbling in this area (psychotherapy) causes negative outcomes and may, God forbid, lead to suicide," and, "before telling people with phobias, depression and obsessive-compulsive disorders to consult their rabbis and not their psychologists, success rates for rabbis for particular conditions ought to be objectively assessed and published."[1]

Several actual examples of negative outcomes as a result of "amateur dabbling" by rabbis are presented below.

1. A woman who was hospitalized several times in a psychiatric hospital with a diagnosis of schizophrenia was told by a well-known kabbalist with whom she had consulted, that the voices she hears was that of an angel who was punishing her for her transgressions and that she should repent. This declaration was in sharp contrast to her therapist's attempts to convince the patient that the voices she hears were imaginary and that this was her way of attempting to deal with her unacceptable thoughts and feelings. While the former was reinforcing the patient's pathology and guilt feelings, the latter was attempting to help the patient strengthen her ability to test reality and diminish her intense guilt feelings and suicidal ideations.
2. A father consulted his rabbi regarding his daughter who was suffering from depression and was not functioning for over a year. The rabbi cautioned the father against consulting a psychiatrist and advised him to change the mezzuzot in his house. When his daughter's condition didn't improve after he acquired new mezzuzot, the father sought professional help.
3. A student sought his rabbi's advice regarding his un-certainty about marrying his fiancée after he noticed that she was extremely preoccupied with cleanliness (she avoided touching objects that fell on the floor, spent considerable time washing, etc.). The rabbi assured his student that his fiancée would stop this "foolishness" after her marriage. A month after the wedding, the student's wife was hospitalized with a diagnosis of severe obsessive-compulsive disorder and a year later, the couple separated.[2]

Clergymen and clinicians have something of value to offer to each other to enhance the quality of their assistance to the people they serve. Therefore it is extremely important that both professions recognize the limits of their own professional competence and consider the benefits of working and consulting with each other.

Interdisciplinary collaboration between clergymen and mental health practitioners—especially psychotherapists—in treating emotionally disturbed patients is a rare phenomenon. One explanation for this is the relative ignorance of and unfamiliarity with each other's field and area of concern. This tends to produce anxiety, doubt, suspicion, and mutual distrust.

Bi-directional programs of education and collaboration should be developed and offered to clergymen and clinicians.[3] By providing clergy with some basic knowledge and exposure to psychopathology and psychiatric and psychological treatment, they will develop a greater appreciation for the complexity of the human mind and psychotherapy, and will be in a better position to make more appropriate referrals and provide supportive counseling to their emotionally disordered and distressed parishioners.[4] Likewise, a basic knowledge of religious laws, customs, values and rituals will enable psychotherapists to better appreciate the benefits of religious belief and conduct to mental health and make more effective and appropriate diagnoses, referrals and interventions in their clinical work.

In regards to the latter point, the potential deleterious effect of a significant lacuna in the knowledge of religious laws and rituals of the clinician, was demonstrated recently during a staff conference. The intaker presented a case of a religious patient "who compulsively mumbled a prayer about holes and orifices after exiting from the lavatory." Several staff members opined that the patient was psychotic and recommended that he be given anti-psychotic medication until a more enlightened staff member explained that religious Jews recite a prayer after relieving themselves, thanking God for his wisdom in creating man.

In response to the above recommendation, a pilot program was recently initiated at Kaplan Hospital by the authors. A prominent communal rabbi was invited to deliver a series of lectures to the mental health staff of the hospital (psychiatrists, psychologists, psychiatric social workers, psychiatric nurses, vocational and rehabilitation therapists and medical and psychology students training at the hospital) on "Mental Health and Judaism." Issues discussed including Judaism's view of and attitude towards the mentally ill, the halachic status of the mentally ill, the role of the rabbi in dealing with emotionally distressed and disturbed people, areas of conflict between rabbis and mental health practitioners, rabbis' attitude toward psychiatric and psychological treatment and cooperation between the two disciplines. These lectures were highly informative and produced spirited give and take between the speaker and the audience.

A series of ten lectures on various aspects of mental health was initiated by the authors for local clergymen. Topics included psychopathology, psychiatric and psychological treatment, re-habilitation and clergy-clinian cooperation. Twenty rabbis (which included mostly teachers and several community rabbis and Roshei Yeshivot) attended the lectures that were given by various mental health professionals (psychiatrists, psychologists, and social workers) from the hospital staff and other lecturers. The participants were asked to fill out a "feedback" questionnaire after each lecture and at the conclusion of the course.

The following is a summary of their responses:

To the question, "To what extent the course contributed to your understanding of the subject?", and "To what extent the course was important or interesting?" ninety-five percent of the respondents answered "very much." Seventy percent were of the opinion that the course helped them "very much" to clarify their position and attitude toward the subject, ninety percent were "very much" interested in additional lectures on the subject and one hundred percent stated that they would recommend that rabbis participate in similar courses. Sixty percent expressed the opinion that as a result of the course, they had a more positive attitude toward the subject of mental health and were more willing to refer people to mental health practitioners. Eighty percent were glad that the course was "for rabbis only" and were interested in participating in ongoing group consultation meetings with a mental health professional.

It is recommended that similar programs be initiated by mental health practitioners for the benefit of rabbis, clinicians, and the people they serve.[5]

Comments by Rabbi Naphtali Bar-Ilan, Community Rabbi of Rehovot, Israel.

I have strong reservations about the author of the article ("Increasing Clergy–Clinician Cooperation") determining that ultra-orthodox rabbis generally regard psychiatry as a threat to religion and its values. In the book, "Hatora Hamesamachat", written by Yoseph and Ruth Eliyahu and approved by Rabbi Avigdor Nebenzahl, who was one of the outstanding students of Rabbi S. Z. Auerbach, z"l, we found that Rabbi Auerbach, when asked about a young couple that needed the intervention and treatment of a non-observant psychologist, determined that "not only is it permitted but it also is a mitzvah" (page 155). This was his decision after he examined in detail the nature of the psychologist's method.

What is more, we have found that ultra-orthodox rabbis have often determined that psychological treatment is a matter of saving a soul and in some cases have even permitted the patient to transgress certain prohibitions when it was an essential part of the treatment process.

I cannot accept the basic division between rabbis identified as ultra-orthodox and those referred to as modern-orthodox. They both prefer referring, in the first place, to G-d fearing psychologists and psychiatrists who identify with the patient's religious beliefs. However, when this is impossible, they both permit referring people in need of psychological treatment to non-observant psychologists on condition that they promise to refrain from dealing with matters of beliefs and observance.

NOTES

1. D Greenberg and E Witztun. Editorial: "Ultra-orthodox Jewish attitudes toward mental health care". *Israel Journal of Psychiatry Related Sciences*, 31, no. 3 (1994): 143–44.

2. It recently came to our attention that a new, innovative program was recently initiated by a group of haredi rabbis and religious mental health practitioners from Jerusalem (רפואה על פי הלכה - רפע"ה), to aid sufferers of obsessive-compulsive disorders, from the religious-haredi community. The organization had published a pamphlet explaining the disorder and its treatment and also offers free consultation to sufferers of O.C.D. via the telephone or fax).

3. B Lichner-Ingram, D Lowe. "Counseling activities and referral practices of rabbis". *Journal of Psychology and Judaism* 13, no. 3 (1989): 133–48.

4. Rabbi Shlomo Wolbe, a prominent haredi rabbi, author and educator living in Israel, wrote in an article ("Psychiatry and Religion" in "In the Pathways of Medicine," 5 Sivan, 5749 (Hebrew)), "there is an urgent need to organize courses for practicing rabbis and educators, in order to disseminate basic knowledge of the symptoms of neurosis and psychosis and their treatment, in order that they will know to refer mentally ill people immediately to the psychiatrist. Basic knowledge will remove many prejudices."

5. Recently, "Moreshet Yaacov", Religious Teachers' College of Jewish Studies in Rehovot, added the course, "Introduction to Mental and Behavioral Disorders", to their B. Ed. Program.

Chapter Two

Accidental Death: A New Look At an Ancient Model

Judith Guedalia, Ph.D., Yocheved Debow, M.A. and David Debow

PROPOSAL

For the accidental killer—a person who inadvertently caused the death of another human being—the aftermath of the fatal accident is overwhelmingly painful. Accidental death occurs frequently; traffic and military accidents often claim fatalities. Such death becomes a double-edged tragedy, for both the bereaved family and the accidental perpetrator, whose experience often sentences him/her to a lifetime of turmoil. The Bible discusses the concept of a "City of Refuge" (Hebrew: Ir Miklat), a sanctuary to protect the accidental killer, who was to move to one of these forty-eight cities and live there for an indeterminate period of time (Exodus 21:12–14; Numbers 35:9–29; Deuteronomy 4:42; 19:1–13) We suggest that an analysis of the guidelines and directives clearly stated in the Bible and Rabbinical commentaries may not only provide insight into the psychological trauma experienced by an accidental killer but also help provide ideas for a contemporary rehabilitation model. We have selected concepts from studies of Post-Traumatic Stress Disorder (PTSD) and have also used the diagnostic framework of the Diagnostic and Statistical Manual of Mental Disorders, Fourth Edition (DSM-IV). Moreover, we examine the Ir Miklat (IM) from a psychological perspective. It is our contention that the IM concept can serve as a model for understanding the effects of accidental death on the accidental killer (or, in the words of the Bible, 'Rotzeah Beshegaga', hereafter RB), his/her family and the surrounding society.

PURPOSE

Accidental death is a frightening prospect, as it may occur to anyone. Most people would like to believe in the orderliness of events in this world, yet accidental deaths occur under many different circumstances. Recently, the secrecy surrounding incidents of accidental killing in the Israeli Defense Forces has been lifted. Live ammunition is used regularly in training exercises, and the dangers of accidental killing in the army are felt more acutely than in everyday life. Nevertheless, newspapers are filled with reports of fatal traffic accidents, which are the major locus of accidental killing. From 1982 to 1992 in Israel alone there were 4879 people killed in traffic accidents.[1] An extensive search for empirical data, including a computer search of the psychological literature since 1987, revealed only twenty-four papers mentioning accidental killing. Of these, not one dealt directly with the impact of accidental killing on the person who caused it. It thus emerges that despite the large number of people facing this tragedy and the ensuing distress, attempts at helping the perpetrators of accidental killing face their own future are insufficient. In searching for a model, we examined the IM concept presented in the Bible

IR MIKLAT

The Ir Miklat (IM), or City of Refuge, is a Biblical concept described in several Biblical texts (Exodus 21:12–14; Numbers 35:9–29; Deuteronomy 4:42; 19:1–13) as a city to which an accidental killer could flee to escape the vengeance of the victim's family. The plan as described in the Bible calls for six such cities to be set up, specifically dedicated to being Cities of Refuge (Numbers 35:6). Another forty-two cities, which were set aside for the Levites to live in, were also available to be used as Cities of Refuge[2] for Israelites who had committed an accidental killing. Immediately after the accident, before a court had decided whether the death indeed conformed with the legal definition of "accidental killing," the perpetrator would flee to an IM and would be protected within the clearly marked boundaries of this 'sanctuary'. S/he would thus no longer be vulnerable to 'blood avengers', family members of the deceased who would not be tried for murder if they took the life of the accidental killer outside an IM (Numbers 35:27). Rabbinical sources and biblical commentators, who continually re-evaluate and re-interpret the biblical sources, have endeavored to find a precise legal definition of accidental killing. It is distinguished from criminal negligence on the one hand and total circumstantial involvement on the other. In this paper we are discussing the 'inadvertent' homicide-homicide in which there is a slight degree of negligence. Once a person was adjudicated an accidental killer, s/he was permitted to live in the IM and continue his/her normal existence there. The exact time of release was arbitrary, as it depended on the death of one of the three High Priests who functioned at any given time. Only then was the accidental killer permitted to leave the IM and return to his/her previous home (Exodus 35:25. It is this concept of Ir Miklat that we wish to explore.

THE ACCIDENTAL KILLER—'ROTZEACH BISHGAGA'

In any fatal accident, the focus is usually on the deceased and his/her relatives. However, there is often someone who feels responsible for having caused the death, however unintentionally.[3] There are many and varied types of situations in both army and civilian life which can lead to accidental killing. A search of papers published in psychological journals since 1987 reveals almost no literature dealing with the problem of the accidental killer. One book, Fatal Moments,[4] is based on interviews conducted from 1980 to 1990 with nearly 200 people who responded to their call to explore this phenomenon. The study presents the following model of the experience of the accidental killer, claiming that, despite some individual variation, most accidental killers experience a similar pattern of responses. Generally, psychological shock comes first. During this brief period of numbness, the mind hides from the full realization that one has caused the death of another human being. This is followed by preoccupation with the accident. In the struggle to make sense of the event, many accidental killers replay it over and over in their minds. Anger often engulfs the accidental killer, directed at every aspect and player in the accident, including the victim. Guilt is nearly universal, causing accidental killers to torture themselves for unfounded reasons as well as for error and oversight. Depression, also common, may occur in various forms. Their internal turmoil may cause them to withdraw from family and friends and keep them from normal social interaction. They usually experience some form of social tension, often resulting from the failure of their friends and associates to respond or act supportively, due to their unfamiliarity with the situation. Family stress occurs as well. At some point, virtually all accidental killers begin the process of healing. Nevertheless, the aftermath of the event extends throughout their lives.[5] Thus most accidental killers themselves become victims of the event. All the symptoms experienced by accidental killers are included in the definition of Post-Traumatic Stress Disorder. DSM-IV[6] lists several diagnostic criteria for PTSD:

A. The person has been exposed to a traumatic event in which both of the following were present:
 1) The person experienced, witnessed or was confronted with an event or events that involved actual or threatened death or serious injury, or a threat to the physical integrity of self or others;
 2) The person's response involved intense fear, helplessness, or horror.
B. The traumatic event is persistently re-experienced in one (or more) of the following ways
 1) Recurrent and intrusive distressing recollections of the event, including images, thoughts or perceptions.
 2) Recurrent distressing dreams of the event.
 3) Acting or feeling as if the traumatic event were recurring (including a sense of reliving the experience, illusions, hallucinations, and dissociative flashback episodes.
 4) Intense psychological distress at exposure to internal or external cues that symbolize or resemble an aspect of the traumatic event.
C. Persistent avoidance of stimuli associated with the trauma and numbing of general responsiveness, as indicated by three or more of the following:
 1) Efforts to avoid thoughts, feelings, or conversations associated with the trauma;
 2) Efforts to avoid activities, places, or people that arouse recollections of the trauma;
 3) Inability to recall an important aspect of the trauma;
 4) Markedly diminished interest or participation in significant activities;
 5) Feeling of detachment or estrangement from others;
 6) Restricted range of affect;
 7) Sense of a foreshortened future (for example, does not expect to have a career, marriage, children, or a normal life span).
D. Persistent symptoms of increased arousal.
E. Duration of the disturbance is more than one month.
F. The disturbance causes clinically significant distress or impairment in social, occupational, or other important areas of functioning. There are so many stimuli that can engender an emotional reaction that it is hard to avoid the cues that evoke the memory of the trauma.[7] A study of police officers who had witnessed or taken part in shooting incidents found that many suffered from a reaction that took the form of severe PTSD symp-

toms.[8] It would indeed seem that these people have experienced a psychologically distressing event and that their reactions often fit the DSM-IV criteria of PTSD listed above. Although recent research indicates that all these symptoms are usually experienced at the same time, it is still interesting to note the similarities with the classic model of the stages of mourning described in Kubler-Ross's seminal work.[9] There is a difference only in the final stage: 'aftermath' in accidental killing and 'acceptance of death' in the Kubler-Ross model. We propose that what may make it difficult for RBs to experience 'acceptance' in any way may be that they actually remain in the state of mourning. They are mourning not only for the victim who actually died but also for themselves, who are still alive, but no longer in their former state of innocence—the person they were before the fatal moment. At some point RBs apparently realize that they can never be this old self again; the moment of accidental killing has irrevocably changed them and in a certain way perhaps "deadened" an innocent and unburdened self. Thus they may actually be mourning for the person they can no longer be. Shalev[10] offers a psychodynamic formulation of PTSD as "incomplete processing of traumatic experiences similar to pathological mourning." Although he considers this definition insufficient to encompass the full nature of PTSD, it could certainly serve as a partial explanation of the psychic processes occurring in the PTSD patient, particularly the RB. Accidental killers are frequently acquitted in court for the crime of manslaughter. Legal exoneration, however, cannot reverse the accident and return the dead person to life, nor can it render the RB a person who has not killed anyone, albeit accidentally. Often, an RB's reaction after being acquitted is to say that the person is still dead, and "it was still my finger on the trigger."[11] Although the law has judged them to be not guilty, their own acute awareness of loss prevents them from accepting that judgment. The RB is no longer the same person s/he was before the event and must spend time mourning the loss of his/her former, "untainted" self. The importance of allowing accidental killers to experience these feelings of guilt has recently been recognized. Terr,[12] in her book on psychic trauma in childhood, emphasizes the importance of guilt as an adaptive mechanism. It allows trauma victims to feel that they had a certain amount of control, even in a situation in which their control was actually minimal. The event can then be faced and worked through. Where there is no working through of the guilt, shame frequently becomes the predominant emotion. It is usually compounded by feelings of helplessness, which make it more difficult for victims to forgive themselves and move on to redefinition and acceptance of the self.[13]

IR MIKLAT—AN UNDERSTANDING BASED ON THE BIBLICAL TEXT AND COMMENTARIES

The Biblical injunction ordering RB's to proceed to an IM contains highly specific directives: All homicides, whether inadvertent or not, fled to an IM and were then brought back to their own town for trial. An RB had to immediately leave the environment in which s/he was living and go to the nearest City of Refuge. Inherent in the command is the immediacy and specificity of the directive. It is imperative to gather oneself together and proceed actively. At every intersection there were signs pointing to the nearest IM, so that it was always accessible. The IM was inhabited by members of the Tribe of Levi and accidental killers. Traditionally, the Levites had no land of their own, thereby freeing them from agricultural responsibilities. Instead, they were the teachers and the social workers, the caretakers of the nation. Their life was dedicated to the soul and spirit of the people, and it would seem that part of their responsibility was to live in the Cities of Refuge, perhaps as the "support staff" for those RBs who needed moral support during healing.[14] It is explained that the city must be neither too large nor too small.[15] This ensured a sense of community, while guaranteeing the RB privacy as well. Another important structural feature was that RBs were never to be a majority of the population.[16] This stricture kept the population healthy and prevented the group malaise that might otherwise be self-perpetuating. The number of people suffering from trauma was never so large that the support mechanism could not function efficiently. The city always had a group of empathic people who were not caught up in working the land, but were free to be helpful and supportive as necessary.

Once an RB was sentenced to spend time in an IM, he would not go there alone; he was encouraged to move there with his family and a "Rabbi" or mentor. (Here we must use the masculine form, as apparently the rule that the RB's family and mentor must accompany him to the IM applied only to males. The husbands of female RB's were enjoined to continue supporting them, but they were not required to accompany them to the IM. Thus women in this position were given some support, but not as much as men; it is the model as proposed for males that we suggest for emulation.) The RB was to be separated from his previous life, but only partially. Perhaps "relocation" would be a more appropriate term. Clearly, the resettlement of the teacher and family would be difficult, yet it was essential for maintaining the RB's existence. The importance of taking along parts of one's former life to the IM was understood. Perhaps another purpose was to make sure the RB would not be able to cloak himself in secrecy. On his arrival in an IM he was announced as an RB.[17] This publicity was not a public branding of shame, but rather meant for the purpose of integration. While the RB was not required to part from his immediate family, the act of relocation clearly separated him from the rest of society. This might have helped prevent the RB from sensing social tension in those around him. Finally, the "release time" for a RB's from the IM was always dependent on an arbitrary event—the death of the High Priest. The random nature of the accident is reflected in the release, which is similarly out of the RB's control.

HOW THE IR MIKLAT MODEL ADDRESSES THE SYMPTOMS OF PTSD

Current models for the explanation and treatment of PTSD are generally found to be unsatisfactory.[18] The complexity of PTSD symptoms seems to call for a multi-dimensional approach. Although this is generally agreed on in theory, much of the literature based on clinical work relies on one-dimensional approaches, and so there is a great deal of dissatisfaction with treatment results.[19] There is still widespread debate about the various treatment options for PTSD, but what seems clear is that an effective treatment model must be multi-dimensional. The literature on PTSD generally states that avoiding situations similar to the one that caused the trauma or attempting to deny the event gives rise to the most severe PTSD symptoms.[20] However, attempting to force the trauma victim to place himself in this type of situation may further exacerbate the symptoms. What is healing is an attempt to treat the psychological reactions to the trauma with a cognitive approach as soon as possible and encourage the trauma victim to face the situation.[21] Seligman in his study of "learned helplessness," described how his experimental subjects learned to be passive when they came to believe that they were unable to control their environment.[22] Once an event such as an accidental death has occurred, the initial feelings of shock, numbness and preoccupation give rise to a need to escape. This need is satisfied by the injunction to flee to the IM. In a situation of total disorientation and turmoil, fleeing to the IM gave accidental killers a way of mobilizing their energy in defense of the ego, thus helping them avoid the internal dialogue of self-defeating talk in which such people may become mired.[23] It forced them into action, which can give one a certain sense of control. This commandment also helped reorient the RB; s/he realized that s/he was not the only accidental killer in the world; the signposts put him/her into a new category with others, so that s/he could redefine him/herself and not feel so alone. The IM thus addresses the unavoidable change in self-concept following trauma, a notion that is often a basis for modern-day dynamic psychotherapies for PTSD. Thus, although RBs were running 'away' from the scene of the trauma, they were also running 'towards' a place that would redefine them specifically through this trauma, and force them to face the consequences of their acts, albeit within a therapeutic and supportive setting. This combination of running away from the scene of the crime, while running towards a place where help could obtained, creates an apparently paradoxical combination of avoidance and activity. Activity seems important for giving one a feeling of control over one's body, something RBs may feel they have lost by doing something which seems to have been uncontrolled.[24] In her book describing her work with the Chowchilla children, Terr shows that those who were able to actively do something to try and save themselves from the disaster emerged less traumatized, apparently because they had been active in protecting themselves. She notes in particular that one child, who was explicitly told not to help because he was "too weak and too fat", spent years trying to prepare himself for the next time he could be a "hero" until he died at the age of fifteen in an accident.[25]

Although this is only a single case, it nevertheless supports the contention that being active provides a certain sense of control that facilitates recovery. Activity can also help alleviate the psychological numbing defined as a common symptom of PTSD in DSM-IV (1994). Flooding therapies can exacerbate symptoms by evoking emotions associated with the trauma. However, seemingly unrelated activities can work as occupation therapy to provide inputs that give rise to unassociated feelings. Thus allowing the person to have safe emotional experiences that do not have to be suppressed through numbing. An added function of the signposts placed all over the country, directing people to the IM, might be to desensitize the population in general to the idea of accidental killer and thus facilitate their acceptance within the community. They became a part of people's awareness and thus may have served to minimize the accidental killer's sense of being a 'pariah'. In describing the City of Refuge, the Midrash, a homiletic commentary on the Bible, calls it "a healing for you".[26] This seems to imply an understanding that accidental killers indeed need a place to escape to for the purpose of introspection, far from the normal routine of life, which should help them confront the enormity of the events. The Bible displays sensitivity to the RB's traumatic experience, realizing that under such circumstances people cannot be expected to return to their usual lifestyle without taking time out to work through the trauma. Moreover, being accompanied to the IM by one's mentor and family changed the nature of the exile. Perhaps its purpose was to demonstrate that one's lifestyle should not be altered. There is clear evidence of the importance of family support in facilitating the recovery of trauma victims despite the fact that they cannot always provide all the support a trauma victim needs.[27,28] Another purpose may have been to prevent a reaction that is fairly common in

PTSD—the feeling that the future is foreshortened that there is nothing more to live for, that one's life is basically over.[29] Thus the RB was not allowed to be cut off from his immediate supportive environment, even though he was forced to move away from a society which might well have difficulty taking him back. Since the RB might be unable to face the flooding that often accompanies repeated return to the scene of the trauma[30] he was protected from it at the same time that he was encouraged to face himself and his new identity. In addition, it was recognized that cloaking oneself in secrecy would only foster an unhealthy reaction to the trauma. It was for this reason that the RB's arrival at the IM was announced in advance. The environment did not permit avoidance. This addressed a major symptom of PTSD. As mentioned previously, RBs generally experiences guilt feelings despite legal acquittal. By bringing them to an environment in which they would be with others in a similar situation, the IM directive eased their bewilderment and provided a sense of comfort and fraternity. Family or friends who never had this sort of experience may be unwilling to listen to repeated descriptions of the horrors of the event.[31] Sharing experiences with others in similar circumstances can help the RBs in many ways. It encourages them to confront the fact that they do indeed have a new identity, similar to that of others in the new environment. This confrontation, which may occur in the face of denial, often serves to relieve some of their anxiety by demonstrating that there are other people in the same predicament. This, in turn, may help alleviate guilt feelings. Living in a place with others who may be more advanced in the healing process, can encourage them to face the future. Although separated from their previous way of life and aware that guilt feelings cannot be ignored, the RBs are not alone in their experience and reactions to it. Clearly, sharing these feelings with others and being exposed to others in various stages of recovery from their trauma can facilitate rehabilitation. There are various reports in the literature about the use of group and milieu therapy for the treatment of PTSD, particularly with Vietnam veterans.[32,33] The first of these reports describes a weeklong program for a group of Vietnam veterans at Camp David, an area surrounded by mountains and isolated from nearby towns. The treatment program included traditional treatment methods for PTSD, as well as Native American healing techniques. An evaluation immediately after the program, and a three-month follow-up, indicated significant reduction of symptomatology for nearly every measure of psychopathology.[34]

Another helpful factor is that the IM was primarily inhabited by Levites—an important sector of the community, mentors of the population. Thus the RBs' knowledge that they were not being sent to spend their 'sentence' with a socially undesirable community, but were worthy of the company of the Levites, may also have served to help them re-acquire a favorable sense of identity. It is interesting to note that the Levite community also served a primary role in preparing the sacrifices for the Temple. They were known to be people characterized by great precision.[35] It might also have been important for accidental killers to be exposed to this trait as part of their battle against the randomness of the event that had so dramatically changed them. Finally, there is the arbitrary release time. This awareness of non-control is essential in mitigating the RBs' sense of personal responsibility for themselves and the community, and in facilitating rehabilitation and a return to the larger society.

DISCUSSION

Modern society appears to respond to killing dichotomously—either it is accidental and therefore not punishable, or it is intentional and therefore punishable. Ancient Jewish society added a middle possibility—even if the killing may be accidental, so that the killer is innocent of a crime, s/he is nonetheless responsible for a death, and must therefore be punished. The biblical injunction ordering RBs to proceed to an IM has traditionally been understood as serving as a punishment for the R.B. and a necessary step in facilitating Kapparah for causing, even accidentally, the death of another human.

Today, accidental killers are aware that they have caused someone's death, yet there is no formal reaction from society. The implicit message is that the RBs are not at fault and may therefore disassociate themselves from the tragedy. This situation makes the natural process of mourning and subsequent rehabilitation into society more difficult. It leaves the RBs without the means to integrate this traumatic event into a new personal identity, and thus leads to behaviors that are defined as PTSD symptoms. The palpable result is heightened PTSD. A powerful symptom of PTSD, which exacerbates the RB's suffering, is avoidance.[36] Healing is a long, slow process that comes with introspection and facing the reality of what has happened.[37] The concept of IM provides many lessons. Society needs to separate from the RB, and that the RB needs to be distanced from the physical cues of the environment in which the accidental killing occurred. This relocation permits the RBs to mourn for their old, *unconfounded* self, and construct a new, acceptable personal identity. Being in a supportive and accepting societal environment in which RBs are recognized as such—in this new and as yet *unintegrated* identity—could facilitate their rehabilitation. As the modern outlook appears to recognize formally only one dimension of the situation—guilty as opposed to innocent of a crime—there is no place for the paradoxical psychological needs of the accidental killer. Establishing a middle ground—innocent and yet responsible—accepts the reality that this person's two losses (of the person who was killed as well as his/her own previous 'innocent' self) must be accounted for. This allows RBs to redefine themselves in a way that is congruent with his/her psychological state.

CONCLUSION

The treatment of PTSD remains a challenge for the health profession. The complexity of the disorder underscores the difficulty in establishing a clear treatment of choice, or perhaps a constellation of treatments of choice, for patients suffering from PTSD. Moreover the paucity of literature on the subject of accidental killers reflects the lack of attention given them as a group. Perhaps it is easier for those in the helping professions to comfort and work with "pure victims" rather than "victim-perpetrators". They are, however, undoubtedly people who have undergone a traumatic event, and as such deserve our attention. In this paper we have attempted to present the Biblical model of the Ir Miklat as an all-encompassing approach to the treatment of the specific trauma of accidental killers. Nevertheless, the model as it existed in ancient times clearly cannot be transferred as a whole to modern-day society. It must be kept in mind that an important element in the efficacy of the IM model, which would be difficult to replicate nowadays, is the idea of ritual integral to the procedure. The clearly set out rules and processes were an accepted form enabling RBs to expiate their sense of guilt. At present, when these practices are not accepted by the larger society, there is no prescribed way for RBs to act. However, the model of a separate community can certainly be operationalized today in the form of group homes or special facilities. The experimental model for treatment of Vietnam veterans at Camp David was very similar to the IM model. There are other models for rehabilitation of drug abusers—for example, the Gateway Drug Rehabilitation Clinic in Pittsburgh—which could perhaps serve as a model for creating a rehabilitative environment for RBs. There may even be existing facilities which could be redefined in line with the IM model. The Israel Defense Force presently has a facility that seems to have a similar aim. It could certainly serve as a basis from which to launch a more encompassing model that would take into consideration the various symptoms experienced in PTSD. Although the Levite Tribe no longer serves the functions it had in ancient times, the psychologists and social workers of today could serve similar functions, at least as a therapeutic staff, if not as a community in which RBs could live. The fact that Biblical practice foreshadows many of the same techniques currently used in modern-day psychotherapies for the treatment of PTSD seems to invite using the wisdom of long ago for those who still suffer today as accidental killers.

NOTES AND BIBLIOGRAPHY

1. Ministry of Transportation: Road Safety Authority (1993). Road Safety in Israel: Facts and Figures.
2. M Maimonides, "The Codex of Jewish Law". *Sabbatical and Jubilee Laws* 13:1
3. G Gilliam and BR Chesser, *Fatal Moments: The Tragedy of the Accidental Killer*. (Lexington, Mass.: 1991).
4. Gilliam, *Fatal Moments*
5. Gilliam, *Fatal Moments*
6. American Psychiatric Association. *DSM-IV: Diagnostic and Statistical Manual of Mental Disorders*, Fourth Edition. (Washington, DC: American Psychiatric Association, 1994), 427–428.
7. Keane et al., 1985, quoted in Z Solomon, A Bleich, S Shoham, C Nardi and M Kotler, "The "Koach" Project for treatment of combat-related PTSD: Rationale, aims, and methodology." *Journal of Traumatic Stress*, 5, (1992): 175–193.
8. Heath, BPR Gersons,. "Patterns of PTSD among police officers following shooting incidents: A two-dimensional model and treatment implications." *Journal of Traumatic Stress*, 2, (1989): 247–257.
9. E Kubler-Ross. *On Death and Dying*. (New York: Macmillan, 1969).
10. AY Shalev, "Post-traumatic Stress Disorder: A Biopsychological Perspective". *Israel Journal of Psychiatry and Related Science*, 30, no. 2 (1993): 102–109.
11. The Jerusalem Post (October 1993)
12. L Terr, *Too Scared to Cry*. (New York: Basic Books, 1990).
13. R Janoff-Bulman, *Shattered Assumptions: Towards a New Psychology of Trauma*. (NY: The Free Press, 1992).
14. SR Hirsch, *A Commentary to the Bible*. (1860).
15. M Maimonides, "The Codex of Jewish Law", *Homicide* 8, 8.
16. Maimonides, "The Codex" 7, 6.
17. J Babad, *Minchat Chinuch: A Commentary on the Commandments of the Bible*.
18. AY Shalev, "Post-traumatic Stress Disorder: A Biopsychological Perspective." *Israel Journal of Psychiatry and Related Science*, 30, (2) (1993), 102–109.
19. Shalev, "Post-traumatic Stress".
20. SD Solomon, ET Gerrity and AM Muff, "Efficacy of treatments for Post-traumatic stress disorder: An empirical review". *Journal of the American Medicine Association*, 268, (1992), 633–638.
21. L Terr, *Too Scared to Cry*. (New York: Basic Books, 1990).
22. MEP Seligman, *Learned Helplessness*. (San Francisco: Freeman 1975).
23. Z Solomon, A Bleich, S Shoham, C Nardi, and M Kotler, "The "Koach" Project for treatment of combat-related PTSD: Rationale, aims, and methodology." *Journal of Traumatic Stress*, 5, (1992), 175–193.

24. L Terr, *Too Scared to Cry*. (New York: Basic Books 1990).
25. Terr, *Too Scared to Cry*.
26. *Midrash Devarim Rabbah*
27. JL Herman, Trauma and Recovery. (New York: Basic Books 1992).
28. L Terr, *Too Scared to Cry*. (New York: Basic Books 1990).
29. JL Herman, Trauma and Recovery. (New York: Basic Books 1992).
30. SD Solomon, ET Gerrity and AM Muff, SD Solomon, ET Gerrity and AM Muff, "Efficacy of treatments for Post-traumatic stress disorder: An empirical review". *Journal of the American Medicine Association*, 268, (1992), 633–638.
31. Solomon, "Efficacy of treatments".
32. Wilson (1989)
33. DR Johnson, SC Feldman, SM Southwick and DS Charney, "The Concept of the Second Generation Program in the Treatment of Post-Traumatic Stress Disorder Among Vietnam Veterans." *Journal of Traumatic Stress*, 7, no. 2 (1994).
34. Johnson, "The Concept".
35. M Grodner, *Intention and Homicide in the Talmud*. Unpublished doctoral thesis, (University of Washington, Seattle, 1970).
36. Z Solomon, A Bleich, S Shoham, C Nardi and M Kotler, "The "Koach" Project for treatment of combat-related PTSD: Rationale, aims, and methodology." *Journal of Traumatic Stress*, 5, (1992), 175–193.
37. JL Herman, Trauma and Recovery. (New York: Basic Books 1992).

Chapter Three

Homosexuality: A Religious and Political Analysis

Rabbi Hillel Goldberg, Ph.D.

"Calvin Klein," reads the advertisement. This time, its ritual sexual object is not a woman, nor even a woman in embrace with a man. It is just a man, or, to be more precise, a slice of a man-his chest, breast, arm, stomach. Unclothed, of course.

It does not take a sex or media expert to understand this advertisement's implicit appeal (nor is Calvin Klein its only purveyor).This appeal—the routinization of homosexuality—signals a larger point: American society is now critically close to a line that, if crossed, will forever change the public discussion of homosexuality. Analogously, this is the line that was crossed when controversy over abortion, however bitter or clamorous, became secondary to the reality that abortion could be had without fear of public stigma. When this line was crossed, pro-choice achieved victory in a way far more profound than formal legalization. Once abortion lost its stigma, the very discussion of the issue-even the most coolly cogent or emotionally visceral argument against it-served only to promote it. The critical issue in abortion is the sacredness of life, and once the discussion of the issue became routinized—reduced to the devitalized terminology of law, welfare policy, and medicine-the sacredness was irretrievably attenuated. This facilitated a woman's choice for abortion on demand because even objections to it facilitated its desacralization.

A Catch-22! If one raises no voice against a moral slippery slope, the slope gets steeper, but once a certain massive shift in public consciousness takes place, then to raise a moral voice also steepens the slope. This is why a vigorous analysis of homosexuality is particularly critical now. The issue has come perilously close to that elusive yet decisive line-that breadth of public acceptance, that subtle yet pervasive loss of stigma-on the other side of which any religious or political argument against homosexuality contributes to its routinization. This is not to recommend passivity in the face of analogous moral issues already on the other side of the line. It is to offer the cautiously optimistic estimate that a sustained critique of homosexuality can be not only tenable but effective.

My purpose here is twofold. Religiously, it is to argue that the desire for homosexual sex, however deeply rooted in the psyche and genuinely felt, is not outside the Scope of normative moral definition and correction.

Politically, the purpose is to argue that sexual orientation, legalized as an autonomous civil right, serves to fragment society and ultimately to vulgarize it. By itself, a religious analysis of homosexuality is inadequate. This is because the arguments on behalf of homosexuality are preponderantly psychological. Only a religious framework that has accommodated the fundamental questions of psychology without violating its own integrity can offer an adequate religious analysis of homosexuality. As a rabbi and a student of Musar, the psychological-religious tradition within Judaism, I rely on the Musar tradition in this analysis. By way of brief introduction, Musar literature from its inception in the 10th century until the mid-19th century systematized the psychologically and pietistically charged tales and adages of the Hebrew Bible and the Talmud. This literature promoted character and piety. In the mid-19th century, Musar became a movement among Lithuanian Jewry, only secondarily interested in literary promotion of character and piety. Primarily, Musar evolved a psychology of the unconscious and a range of techniques for understanding and altering the unconscious roots of behavior; and, it regarded religious integrity and psychological health as coextensive. No ritual or ethical act, character trait or attitude could be defined as whole merely for its external loyalty to religious tradition. The unconscious wellsprings of behavior had to be suffused with love of God (in ritual), love of humanity (in ethics), self-transformation (in character), and humility (in attitude).

Essential to this comprehensive integration of religion and psychology was an unfolding of deeper layers of psychological meaning in the tales and adages in the medieval Musar literature. Formative and normative in this psychological unfolding was the Lithuanian Musar movement's founder, Rabbi Israel Salanter (1810–1883), noted Talmudist and pietist. An animating problematic of his religious thought was the retention of responsibility in light of the wildly uncontrollable and unpredictable human psyche. How, Rabbi Israel asked, could God hold people responsible for acting on urges they did not know they had, whose strength they could not assess, and whose etiology they could never be certain they understood? Transposed to the present, how can God (let alone humanity) hold the homosexual responsible for acting on urges he did not suspect he had and whose strength he did not anticipate, as he moved into, and beyond puberty?

The question is compelling for Rabbi Israel because passion and self-deception mark his view of religiously untutored man. As he wrote: "Suddenly man will sin greatly [such that] he cannot morally recoup" and "in a split second man will sin grievously; there is no restraining his spirit, he will execute the most evil and abominable actions under the sun," and in all this he will be unable to "reveal the roots of his heart." To Rabbi Israel, the human heart has unconscious roots that engender unpredictable and disastrous behavior and consist of lusts, wills, urges, and corrupted character traits, all of which Rabbi Israel regarded as connatural. Rabbi Israel never ran dry in describing their malevolence and power, first baldly (as noted), then metaphorically and expositorily. Metaphorically: "Even when evil is uprooted from man's innards, a muddy well remains, hidden in its latency, ready to gush forth its waters under the impact of a great cause . . . that from out of their hiding places the waters reveal themselves, spread out . . . and destroy." Expositorily: "Man cannot grasp the evolution of things . . . because the soul-forces of man proceed in the absence of prevision, from the depths of the heart toward manifestation. . . . Therefore, man, who seeks to comprehend through retroactive observation, will err frequently in his judgment of the roots of the forces. . . . For as long as a force of his soul remains concealed in its roots, as long as it is in hiding from human comprehension, it will continue to shoot its arrows at man's conduct."

Violations of the religious norm that occupied Rabbi Israel were deception, manipulation, thievery, vainglory, anger, and pride. But the question of sexual responsibility is nonetheless reflective of his psychological analysis of the pertinent Talmudic passages. For him, it was axiomatic that while the seedbed of unconscious drives differs from one individual to the next, personal responsibility remains universal. People's unbridled inner desires may differ; their responsibility to work to embody the religious norm to surmount self-deception, corrupted religiosity, and wracking passions remains the same.

Rabbi Israel laid down psychoanalytical, behavioral and group methods that, if diligently practiced over a lifetime, enabled a person to unveil and (if religiously mandated) transfigure the most hidden layers of his unconscious. Ultimately, therefore, a person was responsible for his every violation of the norm, no matter how profound the drive to violate it. Ultimately, in the meantime, God measures each violation of the ritual, ethical, 'character, and attitudinal norm not only, and not even primarily, against its objective magnitude, but against the magnitude of the subjective struggle necessary to prevent it The stronger the inherent drive toward the violation, the greater the Divine mercy toward the violator. The weaker the inherent drive toward the violation, the more severe the Divine judgment of the violator.

The upshot is paradox. Yes, the individual retains responsibility for his every act; but also, the degree of responsibility for every violation of the religious norm is mitigated by the degree of inner resistance to the norm. Yes, the authority of the norm remains in place regardless of time and place; but also, the degree of responsibility for violation of the norm is mitigated by the degree of inner acquiescence to sin occasioned by moral laxity in a particular time and place. The paradox yields both severity and mercy; the religious norm, however onerous, is retained without compromise; God's acknowledgement of the pain in those unable to keep the norm is also retained without compromise.

Rabbi Israel's compassionate theology is mitigated by his observation that sin is often chosen. Unconscious forces, however flagrant, do not rob people of freedom. It is often true that freedom seems delusionary when countless cultural signals-homosexual literature and bars, "gay sensitization" on college campuses, a permissive society generally-validate homosexual desire. It is further true that people, simply by dint of moral decision, cannot often adhere to the religious norm. Even so (wrote Rabbi Israel), people are never robbed of the freedom to choose to undergo therapy empowering them to follow the norm. Masters and Johnson put it this way: "Even if the proportion of genetic or biochemical influences contributing to homosexuality for any individual is equal to or greater than postnatal influences, there is no reason to believe that the fact would specifically deny the possibility of altering the individual's sexual preference." To the extent that people exercise their freedom merely to indulge an inner desire to violate the religious norm, Divine judgment is severe.

Rabbi Israel does not deny the claim that any particular desire to sin might go against "nature." Sin may very well violate a person's sense of his own nature. To Rabbi Israel, nature is nothing more than the unique, individuated constellation of a person's environmental influences and psychic forces, at least some of which are in-born. For a homosexual to claim that his sexual desires define his existence, or, alternatively, to argue that the demand to alter his homosexuality is a reductive attempt to change him into something he is not, would meet no quarrel from Rabbi Israel. He posits that everyone must redefine himself at his very root, moment by moment, that precisely in those specific, unique ways in which a person finds his psychological existence opposed to the religious norm, the individual must change. In terms of psychological principle, it makes no difference to Rabbi Israel whether the in-born desire is for adultery, unethical monetary gain, homosexual sex, or any other violation of the religious norm. The in-born desire-call it "nature" if you will-must be tutored and transfigured.

Correlative to the concept of a complex psyche-an interweaving of conscious and unconscious forces, both chosen and absorbed-is rationalization.

Because a person is rarely true to himself in the sense of accurately knowing the complexity and origins of his own desires, the wrong may seem right, the underlying motivation may be hidden, the stated reason may be spurious. The homosexual desire, for example, may be religiously rationalized as deviating from nothing more than a culturally conditioned norm. The prohibition of homosexuality, it is argued, originated in a morality unable to conceive of love between two people of the same sex. Only loveless, impermanent or coercive homosexuality was prohibited, it is maintained. And yet, Jewish sacred literature divides between the norm that is and is not understandable to human reason, respectively, the mishpat and the hok. The prohibition against homosexuality is a hok, a revelation of the Divine mind, a divine decree independent of any cultural norm. It is true that the human being is expected to grasp the impropriety of homosexuaity intuitively, since the Hebrew Bible labels it to'eva, "abomination"-something that inspires instinctive repugnance. It is also true that the effects of repeated sin, such as homosexual behavior, deaden spiritual sensitivies, "atrophying the heart" (as Rabbi Israel put it), and he whose heart is atrophied cannot intuitively grasp homosexuality's repugnance. Precisely such spiritual atrophy spurs the rationalization of homosexuality. For the rationalizer, the Biblical prohibition will indeed seem to be beyond reason and in that sense, a hok.

However the prohibition of homosexuality is classified-hok, to'eva, or both-the entirety of Jewish sacred literature-Bible, Talmud, kabbala, Musar, philosophy, midrash-sustains the prohibition without any qualification. Intellectual honesty with respect to 3,800 years of Jewish tradition, and the rationalization of homosexuality on religious grounds, do not jibe. The prohibition is absolute, though, as indicated, the corresponding Divine judgment need not necessarily be so.

Let us return to Calvin Klein. Is the homosexual titillation, prompted by the company's advertising, environmentally provoked or individually chosen? Do we deal with a response to an image that, in certain people, elicits erotic thoughts, feelings, or sensibilities; or are these images actively sought for erotic purposes? The two possibilities are not mutually exclusive; their interweaving is symbiotic. The individual, of course, is religiously obligated to transform either source of homosexual desire, whatever the precise proportions of the interweaving. The transformation of homosexual desire should be private and modest, in conjunction with partner(s), therapists and spiritual mentors.

Contemporary reality is just the opposite. Not only is the struggle for transformation not veiled-to be more precise, not only is there little or no struggle at all-but a public agenda would legitimate homosexuality altogether. If religious legitimation is either intellectual dishonesty or subversion of the sacred norm, political legitimation is more complex. Explicitly it is innocent, implicitly not. Explicitly it would merely guarantee the civil rights of individuals, regardless of sexual orientation. The right to be free of harassment, not to mention violence, and the right to live without prejudice, are unexceptionable. The problem is that the explicit political agenda is, and in the nature of things must be, driven by another, far-reaching and implicit agenda.

In essence, the implicit agenda advocates rights for homosexuality, not just for homosexuals. The civil right is linked to the philosophical right. First of all, it is just this way. Homosexual activists support separate legal protection not only on the basis of constitutional theory but also on the basis of psychological, religious, and philosophic justification. Gay rights literature is replete with apologia for homosexuality per se. The message is clear: Rights for homosexuals are meant to pave the way for full legitimation of homosexuality. It is just this way because, in the nature of things, it has to be. If homosexuality is not ingrained and fixed, then there is no basis for legal protection on the basis of sexual orientation. If homosexuality is alterable, it does not merit individuated legal protection any more than any other life-style. To preclude the absurdity of separate legal protection for adulterers or perjurers (for example), homosexuals press the claim that their nature is as indelible as race. Inevitably, a vote for "gay rights" is a vote for homosexuality itself-and it is more.

To consider homosexuals as a distinct legal category contributes to the fragmentation of the body politic. The unnecessary creation of separate categories of citizens before the law erodes social cohesiveness. Homosexuals, it goes without saying, deserve protection of person and property.

The denial of such protection would be unwarranted on constitutional or religious grounds. The democratic system, however, includes equal protection for everyone's person and property. Nothing more is necessary for homosexuals, since discrimination against them is anecdotal, not systematic (on which more below), and since discrimination against them is self-preventable. They need only refrain from verbal or visual announcement their sexual preference, a restraint that does not exclude the private acts they prefer. Thus, while prohibition of discrimination based on race (for example) acknowledges fragmentation in society, such acknowledgement is unavoidable, Race is unavoidably public. Sexual preference can and may be entirely private. Therefore, there is no point to protecting homosexuals publicly, with "gay rights" laws, except to legitimate homosexuality, and there is no consequence of gay rights except to exacerbate divisions in the body politic. The reductio ad absurdum of multiplying special legal designations is to pit one citizen against the other, as each manufactures his own special status and regards it as insufficiently protected. Homosexual rights ordinances are symptomatic of a larger process of social fragmentation that should not be encouraged.

Special legal protection has an unintended consequence: inequality. Special protection is predicated on the assumption that pervasive discrimination exists. When homosexuals keep their private lives private, discrimination, if present at all, is anecdotal, not systematic-and everyone is subject to anecdotal discrimination. But any special category of rights, such as "sexual orientation," presumes the existence of systematic discrimination. When there is none, special legal protection has the paradoxical effect of encouraging those who would harass, injure, or discriminate against the protected party, paradoxically increasing inequality. To be certain, if homosexuality is flaunted, it may elicit bigotry. Self-control, not legal protection, is the solution-just as self-control is the solution for the flaunting of heterosexuality. Vulgarity is not limited to homosexuals, not a variety of victimhood, and not a "right" that freedom of expression protects in an absolute sense, any more than it protects obscenity or "fighting words" absolutely.

Special legal protection reinforces the segregation (or self-segregation) of homosexuals in homosexual groups, bars, churches and synagogues. The "gay synagogue" or "gay church" is particularly disturbing because it is an exercise in inequality in the name of the opposite, an illustration of the fragmentation that "equal protection" ordinances nurture or reflect, a policy that belies the unconditional Divine image and equality of each human being. The strategy of liberal Christians and traditional Jews is to have homosexuals in the standard houses of worship, not to segregate them in separate but equal ones. Rights of free association should not be abrogated, but a social policy that reinforces segregation (or self-segregation) and otherwise is pointless at best-for example, legal protection on the basis of sexual orientation-is divisive.

The homosexual house of worship is the most retrogressive of homosexual institutions because it marks the religious acceptance of homosexuality and the religious inequality of the homosexual-just the opposite of what is religiously required: the rejection of homosexuality and the acceptance of the homosexual. The homosexual house of worship, stigmatizing in accord with sexual preference, is as coherent as "Temple Emanuel: A Heterosexual Congregation." Most serious of all, the assent to segregation in worship is an admission of indifference, tantamount to saying: We prefer not to make the effort to include you or to offer regenerative counseling. We are content for you to remain apart, as you are. A house of worship, however, is for imperfect people seeking holiness and inner healing in conjunction with other imperfect people. To stratify the house of worship on the basis of an imperfection is to bifurcate community. In another age, Otto Kerner issued a warning, "Our nation is moving toward two societies, one black, one white-separate and unequal." Replace "black and white" with "heterosexual and homosexual" for the current disfiguration.

Inclusiveness is not a matter of accepting a status-a deviant sexual orientation—but of accepting a person, and the house of God may not put any qualification on that acceptance. Every sinner-that is, everyone-must be welcome in that house. By the same token, the house of God may neither accept nor acknowledge any permanent spiritual attenuation as a condition for participation. "Homosexual family" membership and "commitment" rites for homosexuals, not to mention openly practicing homosexual clergy, attenuate and qualify the universality of abnegation and the totality of confession that are the heart of Divine-human encounter. The intent of the house of worship-the embrace of the family of man-and the pedagogy of the house of worship-the nurture of the individual family-must be allowed to limn a single trail. They can do so only under the authority of an uncompromised religious norm.

Such a norm is not oppressive. It is demanding. The difference is the difference between the children of privilege who taste every luxury and savor none, and between the children of poverty who struggle for a single dignity and savor it infinitely. It is the difference between a seditious submission to "nature," a spurious parade of "courage," and between Helen Keller's unrealistic rejection of "nature" for genuine triumph. On the one hand, there is the ultimately unbridgeable gulf between the Eternal demand and its ephemeral recipient, with all the majesty attendant upon the struggle. On the other hand, there is the guilt-less, shame-less monochrome of "my own thing"—a thing which, if blessed by the church or synagogue or mosque, or encoded in the law, or sanctified by society, will offer the ease of stasis, the comfort of a category. Safe. Tidy. Secure. "Gay." Bereft of the struggle and the reward of climbing the heights of holiness, of ascending toward He who spoke and the world came into being.

Chapter Four

Rabbinic Insights into Behavior Change

Seymour Hoffman, Ph.D.

This essay will focus on the cognitive-behavioral aspects of the views of several classic Jewish commentators regarding behavior change.

The issue of what causes behavior change in people has been debated for decades. The psychoanalytically oriented practitioners and theoreticians insist that insight is a prerequisite to real change and that change without insight is an illusion. On the other hand, the non-dynamic cognitive-behavioral and strategic therapists argue that enduring behavior and attitude changes are made more likely by first getting a person to engage in new behavior. Insight, in their view, is frequently a by-product, rather than a cause of change.

"Many people who are depressed believe that they "just need to become motivated" but the very symptoms often block such motivation. Therefore, if the person waits to become motivated they wait in vain. Ironically, engaging in an activity even when you feel unmotivated to do so can lead to feeling motivated. We call this working from the outside-in".[1]

The latter view seems to be consistent with that of the author of *Sefer Ha'Hinukh*, who in explicating the 613 Commandments makes the point many times that "one's heart is influenced by one's actions."

Similar views are found in the Talmud. "Rabbi Judah said, 'Man should always occupy himself with learning Torah and its Commandments, even for ulterior motives, for eventually he will do it for idealistic reasons'"[2]

In his commentary to the *Ethics of the Fathers* Maimonides[3] recommends that a person who wishes to dispense a large sum of money for charity should dispense it in small amounts rather than in one large sum, in order that the trait of generosity become instilled in him or her.

(Likewise, Milgram points out in his classic study on obedience that prohibited and evil behavior, when repeated, tends to become the norm. "Once the individual has begun to do evil, he continues doing evil, rather than say to himself, 'Everything I have done to this point is bad and now I acknowledge it by breaking it off' ".[4]

The Talmud says, "If a person transgresses a prohibition and repeats it, it becomes to him permissible").[5]

The concepts of cognitive transformation and cognitive dissonance were also used by the rabbis in understanding and modifying human behavior. Ibn Ezra, in discussing the Tenth Commandment, "Thou shalt not covet . . . your neighbor's wife" states:

Many people will be puzzled by this command. Is it conceivable that there should exist a man who does not, at some time or another, covet a beautiful object? Let me now give you a parable. A country yokel in his right senses will not covet a beautiful princess, since he knows it is impossible to possess her, just the same as he will not seriously desire to have wings like a bird. For this reason the thinking person will neither desire nor covet. Since he knows that the A-lmighty has forbidden him his neighbor's wife, such a course of action will be even further from his mind than from that of the country yokel in regard to the princess.[6]

By viewing his neighbor's wife as even more inaccessible than a princess (cognitive transformation) man can control his desires and train himself not to covet.

In the Tractate Avodah Zara,[7] it is recorded that when Rabbi Akiva saw the beautiful wife of the wicked Tornosrophus, he spat, laughed and cried. The Talmud explains that the reason that Rabbi Akiva spat was that he was repulsed by the thought that she came from a putrid drop of semen. By focusing on this thought, Rabbi Akiva was able to negate, nullify and counter his illicit and unacceptable feelings thoughts and impulses.

Cognitive dissonance is a state in which a discrepancy exists between perception and expectation or precepts and concepts.[8] This situation motivates cognitive processes and defense mechanisms. There exists a strong human drive to reduce dissonance and resolve internal conflict by changing one's view or behavior to conform with one's statements and actions.

Examples of cognitive dissonance are found in the rabbinic literature. In Genesis Rabba[9] Joseph's behavior toward his brothers is discussed:

Simon incited his brothers against Joseph and also threw him in a pit. Since Joseph wanted to uproot the hatred and resentment he felt toward Simon, he [Joseph] catered to all his [Simon's] physical needs by providing him with food and drink, and he bathed and applied ointment to his body.

The rabbis comment that "An action retrains behavior and thought. A thought does not retrain behavior or thought."[10] If one really wants to uproot an evil thought or feeling toward another, he has to do a benevolent act.

The Talmud sages ruled that if one is presented with a situation in which at the same moment a friend's animal is lying under its burden and an enemy needs help in loading his animal, one is obligated to first aid the latter, in order to subjugate the evil impulse.[11] Removing hatred from one's heart is a greater deed than relieving the suffering of an animal. By creating cognitive dissonance between negative feeling (hatred) and positive action (providing service) one is forced to change one's feelings to conform to one's behavior.

Another example of the above is the story about Rabbi Israel Lipkin (Salanter), founder and spiritual father of the "Musar" movement, who while riding in a train, was treated in a disrespectful and abusive manner by a fellow passenger. Upon learning later on that the object of his abuse was the revered Rabbi Lipkin, the young man apologized profusely and asked the rabbi for his forgiveness. Rabbi Lipkin informed him that he forgave him immediately and then proceeded to help him in various ways. When asked by his bewildered disciples why he displayed such kindness to a person who previously insulted and abused him, the rabbi explained that he wasn't sure that he totally forgave the young man, and by helping him, he was able to rid any remnants of anger and resentment towards him.

Jewish religious leaders, moralists, and commentators have always been acute observers of humanity. An analysis of their recommended techniques for interpersonal behavior, self-control, and behavior change may well be a practical contribution to contemporary psychology and psychotherapy.[12]

NOTES

1. CR Martelle, ME Addis and NS Jacobson, *Depression in Context* (New York: W.W. Norton, 2001).

2. Talmud Nazir, 23b.

3. Mishna Avot, 3:15.

4. M Milgram. *Obedience to Authority: An Experimental View* (New York: Harper & Row, 1974).

5. Talmud Yoma, 86b.

6. Ibn Ezra, on Exodus, 20:14.

7. Talmud Avodah Zara, 20a.

8. L Festinger, *A Theory of Cognitive Dissonance* (Evanston, IL: Row, Peterson & Co., 1957).

9. Genesis Raba, 91:8.

10. Talmud Kiddushin, 59b.

11. Talmud Bava Metsia, 32b.

12. S Schimmel, "Free-will, Guilt and Self-control in Rabbinic Judaism"in *Judaism and Contemporary Psychology* 26, no. 4 (1977): 418–29.

Chapter Five

Helpmates: Mother and Father as Co-therapy Model

Seymour Hoffman, Ph.D.

Jewish biblical commentators throughout the centuries have given us keen insights into the psychological makeup of marriage. This may be seen by studying commentary on the second half of Genesis 2:20, "But for Adam there was not found a helpmate for him" For "helpmate" the Hebrew text uses the two words, "ezer k' negdo". The root of "neged" means "opposite" or "against."

The Netsiv (Rabbi Naftali Tsvi Yehuda Berlin, 1817-1893) comments, "Adam understood after he realized his limitations that he needed a helpmate with forces, but oppositional forces that would be a help to him (ezer k'negdo), a help if she is against him-to moderates his traits, and in this manner together they will achieve completeness."

On this same verse Rabbi Samson Raphael Hirsch (1808-1888) comments, "Because the wife is to be the helpmate of her husband, she must be opposite him; because she is to complement him, she must have different characteristics than his."

Nahmanides (Rabbi Moshe ben Nahman, (1194-1270) interprets ezer k'negdo as "opposite, distinct from."

The above insights are further analyzed and explicated by the popular psychology author and psychotherapist, Sheldon Kopp.[1] Reflecting the prevalent views of social scientists today, Kopp says that to some extent people marry to make up for their own deficiencies. We seek the missing half of ourselves, our missing rib. Each of us is in some measure incomplete, with some aspects of our humanity overdeveloped and other aspects neglected. An aggressive person seeks a gentle person; a spontaneous spirit seeks a stable anchor.

If people married spouses just like themselves, disasters might well ensue. Two timid souls would justify each other's cautiousness until neither ventured anything new. An adventuresome pair might escalate each other's recklessness into a spiral of catastrophes.

The differences between spouses are both the strength of a good marriage and the hazards of a bad one. Ironically, we marry the other because he (she) is different from us, and then we complain that he (she) is not like us. We complain bitterly about having to live with a mate who is acting exactly in the way that he (she) found most attractive during courtship! Regarding the latter, the remark by the preeminent biblical commentator Rashi (Rabbi Shlomo Yitshaki, 1040- 1105) on the phrase ezer k'negdo is relevant: "A help against him, i.e., if he is worthy, she will be a help; if not, she will be against him."

Sforno (1470-1550) interprets k'negdo to mean "the opposite end of a scale; equal in value and in dignity." Man and woman have equal worth, though different qualities and functions. Husband and wife contribute their unique genetic makeup to their offspring as well as their unique personality traits. The child, whether he likes it or not, is influenced by the contrasting attitudes and behaviors of his parents towards him (her) and by significant people in his (her) environment.

Mother and father represent two forces, two models for relationship. In the Jewish tradition, the mother expresses unconditional love and acceptance, providing the child with emotional encouragement and support, while the father expresses expectation, responsibility, limitations, and discipline. The former fulfills the nurturant role; the latter, the instrumental role. The former provides the child's emotional needs to cope with the challenges and demands of life; the latter, the tools. Both contrasting influences are vital to assuring that the child grows up physically and emotionally healthy, well adjusted, mature, moral, successful, and contented.[2]

The "Ktav Sofer" (Abraham Sofer, 1815–1871), in his commentary on the book of Shemoth, makes a similar observation regarding the two leaders ("parents") of the Jewish people, Moses and Aaron.

"The redemption required two leaders, each with a different personality. In order to speak to the hearts of the children of Israel that they will believe in the redemption, required a messenger with a good temperament who would comfort the people, sweeten their difficulties, strengthen their spirit and hope for redemption. For this, Aaron stood out, since he would be listened to because he was accepted by the people, because he loved and pursued peace. In contrast, in external affairs with Pharaoh, a messenger with strong will power and endurance that fulfills his task fearlessly, is required. For this, Moses stood out, for he spoke to Pharaoh impudently: "In order that thou know that the earth is the Lord's" (Shemoth, 9, 29); "Thou must also give into our hand sacrifices and burnt-offerings" (Shemoth, 10, 25); I will see thy face again no more" (Shemoth, 10, 29).

DIALECTICAL CO-THERAPY

The above insights and views gave birth to the development of a psychotherapeutic approach known as "dialectical co-therapy." This approach exploits the different and contrasting traits and functions of co-therapists in their simultaneous treatment of individuals, couples, and families.[3]

The two dialectical co-therapists working together take consistently opposing views, functions, and roles from the beginning of treatment until positive change has been realized. One therapist is supportive, nurturing, and empathic, while the other therapist is provocative, confronting, and challenging. The former relates to the affective needs, wishes, and fantasies of the client(s), encouraging their strengths and positive attributes, while the latter is instrumental and reality orientated, prompting the client(s) to cope and change.

According to psychotherapist Marcia Linehan, "dialectics" refers to the process of change that occurs through the simultaneous considerations of opposing viewpoints.[4] Haim Omer views dialectical interventions as "treatment strategies that embody two antithetical moves in such a way that as the pendulum swings from one side to another, change forces are mobilized and resistances neutralized. These interventions consist of two coordinated contrary movements that may be thought of as a thesis and an antithesis. Although sometimes the intervention aims at giving maximum power to one of the polar movements, at other times, it aims at an emerging synthesis."[5]

Regarding the above treatment approach, psychologist Brurit Laub has suggested a model that deals with the application of the universal polarity to the therapeutic situation. "Polarity is a central concept in Eastern and Western cultures. The concept of polarity is one of the main elements in the Kabbalah and is described as the male element (right side) and the female element (left side)."[6]

The tasks and goals of parents as well as psychotherapists are to provide their charges with positive, constructive, and appropriate guidance, counsel, support, encouragement, and tools so that their children/clients can lead productive self-fulfilling lives, contributing to their family and society.

Bill Roller and Vivian Nelson point out that the qualities and givens vital for co-therapists to succeed are identical to those for parents:

1. Dual sex-two distinctly different positive role models with whom to identify
2. Style and personality-different and complementary
3. Theoretical orientation-different but flexible

4. Relationship-egalitarian, trusting, non-competitive, cooperative, equal participation and responsibility, openness in communication, mutual support, respect and fondness for each other
5. Goals-the welfare and betterment of their charges[7]

SUMMARY

A successful husband-wife and father-mother relationship of two opposite personalities that attract, complement, and help one another serves as the model for dialectical co-therapy. Both children and therapy clients benefit from receiving the contrasting behaviors of their parents and co-therapists. Since the demands, responsibilities, and challenges are great, choosing the right helpmate is vital.

NOTES

1. SB Kopp, *If You Meet the Buddha on the Road, Kill Him* (New York: Bantam Books, 1972).

2. See Rabbi Yitzchak Shilat, "Cloning in the Light of the Halakha" in Tanhumin, vol. 18, 5758, 141–143 (in Hebrew): "Every child spiritually needs a father and a mother. The father and mother figures are important for the child to identify with in the process of forming his own unique personality. Giving birth to a child into a fatherless family planned in advance and not as a result of the tragic death of the father during pregnancy, G-d forbid, is an injustice to the child, who is destined to grow up with a serious spiritual deficiency. On the other hand, it is permissible for a married couple to bring a child into the world when only his mother is his biological parent . . . because eventually the father will emotionally accept him as a son. If an orphan who is raised in one's home becomes to be like one's son (Talmud Sanhedrin 19b), then all the more so if a couple wants the child and raises him together from birth. In the opinion of psychologists, an orphan who didn't know his father, identifies nevertheless with his father, based on what he hears about him from his mother and others."

3. S Hoffman, S Gafni and B Laub, *Co-therapy with Individuals, Families and Groups* (New Jersey: Jason Aronson, 1994).

4. MM Linehan, *Cognitive-Behavioral Treatment for Borderline Personality Disorder* (New York: Guilford Press, 1991).

5. H Orner, "Dialectical Interventions and the Structure *of* Strategy" in *Psychotherapy,* 28, no. 4, (1991): 563-571.

6. S Hoffman and B. Laub, "Dialectical Cotherapy". *Israel Journal of Psychiatry and Related Sciences,* 41, 3, 2004, 191-196. See also E. Hoffman, *The Way of Splendor: Jewish Mysticism* and *Modern Psychology* (Northvale, NJ: Jason Aronson, 1992) pp. 47–51.

7. B. Roller and V Nelson, *The Art of Co-therapy: How Therapists Work Together* (New York: Guilford Press, 1991).

Chapter Six

Manipulation in Psychological Treatment: Rabbinic View

Seymour Hoffman, Ph.D.

In her review of "Co-therapy with Individuals, Families and Groups" (Israel Journal of Psychiatry, 37, 1, 2000), Rachel Chazan criticized the "dialectical co-therapy approach" that my colleagues and I developed and described in the book, on moral grounds. "It is difficult to accept a method of therapy based on deliberate dishonesty. It is hard to believe that the deception has no long-term ill effects. Even if it succeeds, does the end justify the means"?

According to this view, and there are many practitioner who subscribe to it, treatment approaches that make use of placebos in medical and psychological treatment and paradoxical interventions popularized by such prominent strategic therapists as Haley, Madaness, Frankl, Zeig, Rossi, Lankton, Lustig, and Milton Erickson, to name a few, would be considered "treif", "verboten" and unacceptable.

I would like to respond to the question raised by the reviewer.

Strategic therapy is a direct treatment approach that aims to relieve symptoms, resolve conflicts, and free people from their neurotic morass in the shortest time possible. This approach relies heavily on manipulation to effect change quickly and effectively.

Manipulation in the most concrete sense is the act of controlling with the hands or the mind. The use of manipulation has produced wide debate and heated reaction among psychotherapists of all persuasions.[1,2,3] On the one hand, there are those who decry its use because they think it is patronizing, infantilizing, presumptuous, coercive, deceptive, abusively authoritarian, unethical, inconsistent with respect for the client and incompatible with developing a trusting therapeutic relationship.

On the other hand, there are therapists who argue that "life is one big manipulation" and insist that it is involved in all forms of therapy, ranging from analytically orientated to behavioral and strategic, though it may not be equally obvious in all forms. In their view, manipulation is nothing more than influence, and in therapy, "one cannot not influence" just as "one cannot not communicate". The question is not whether to influence or not but how to do it in the most constructive, humane, non-exploitative, effective, and expeditious manner, in order to effect positive change in the client and help him ameliorate his symptoms and resolve his conflicts. Manipulation in its most benign and simple form is no more complicated than a mother placing a band-aid or a kiss on the wound of a child to "make it all better." In its more complex form, manipulation involves deception and shrewd, devious, and strategic interventions.[4]

Manipulation for therapeutic and altruistic motives has been sanctioned by leading Jewish religious leaders, although it was condemned when used for selfish interests because the values of integrity and honesty are paramount.

(An example of the latter is found in Tractate Yevamot (63a)): "The wife of Rav (one of the outstanding scholars in the Talmudic era, was in the habit of irritating him. When he requested from his wife to cook for him lentils, she cooked for him chick-peas and when he requested chick-peas, she would cook for him lentils. When his son Chiyah grew up, he reversed the requests of his father to his mother. Rav said to his son: 'Your mother has improved'. His son said: 'I am the one that reversed the requests to her'. His father said to him: 'This is what people say, that your son teaches you wisdom. Even so, don't do this, because it is written in Jeremiah, 'Their tongues will teach deceitful things' ").

Rashi in his commentary on *Ethics of the Fathers* (1:2) records the strategic-manipulative interventions of Aaron the High Priest, who antedated Haley and Erickson, two of the most prominent strategic therapists, by 3300 years.

Several examples are given regarding Aaron's manipulative therapeutic methods of intervention:

One man became angry with his wife and chased her out of the house and swore that he would permit her to return only if she spat in the face of the High Priest.

When Aaron became aware of this, he summoned the woman and told her that he had an eye infection which could only be cured if she spat at it. After considerable pleading, the woman acceded to Aaron's request. Afterwards, Aaron summoned the husband and related to him what his wife had done. As a result of this, the couple reconciled. (A similar intervention is recorded in Vayikra Rabba, 15:9).

When two men quarreled, Aaron would go to one of the disputants and inform him that he had just returned from the disputant's friend and found him terribly upset and regretful of the pain that he had caused his fellow. Aaron would not leave the disputant until all jealousy and hatred had been removed from his heart. Afterwards, he would go to the other injured party and repeat the same thing to him. When the men met, they would fall on each other's shoulders and tearfully reconcile.

The most famous and psychologically sophisticated manipulative intervention by a Jewish religious leader recorded in the Scriptures, is described in Kings-1 (3, 15–28), regarding King Solomon's judgment in the dispute between two women contesting the maternity of the live child.

Several examples are recorded in the Talmud of manipulative behavior by prominent religious figures whose intentions were to help fellow Jews. It is related in Tractate Nedarim (50a) that the Prophet Elijah appeared at Rabbi Akiva's dwelling (a barn where he and his wife slept on straw) as a pauper and requested some straw for his wife who had recently given birth to lie down on. Rabbi Nissim explains that Elijah did this in order to console the couple and show them there were people poorer than themselves.

In Tractate Yevamot (11b) it is recorded that the Sages advised a woman to "playact" (to cry, tear her clothing, and dishevel her hair) when she appeared before Rabbi Judah in order to convince him that her husband had died, so that he would permit her to remarry.

In Tractate Arachin (23a), it is related that Moses the son of Etsri was the guarantor for the marriage contract of his daughter-in-law. His son, Rabbi Huna, was wa scholar with little financial resources. Abaye said: "Is there no one to advise Rabbi Huna to divorce his wife and since he is without means, his wife will collect the money from his father and afterwards Rabbi Huna will remarry her. This way he will be able to support her and himself." The Talmud explains that this kind of conspiracy is permissible when it is done for the benefit of a son who is a scholar.

An example of a psychologically more sophisticated intervention by a prominent rabbinic figure of the last century is recorded by Karlinsky.[5] The incident took place in Warsaw in 1877. Rabbi Joseph Dov Soloveitchik, an outstanding Talmud scholar, religious personality, and leader was overcome by a deep depression upon the incarceration of his highly revered and beloved mentor, Rabbi Joshua Leib Diskin, on false charges by the anti-Semitic authorities. On the Sabbath Rabbi Soloveitchik ate only the minimal amount of food necessary to fulfill the requirements of Jewish law. He isolated himself in his room and refused to receive any visitors, not even his closest students and colleagues. He discontinued going to the synagogue and teaching. A specialist who was called in to treat him recommended total rest, but added that if by chance the rabbi's spirit could be suddenly stimulated, healing would take place in a matter of minutes.

Attempts by his family, friends, students, and colleagues to pull him out of his depression failed. Even the efforts of the renowned scholar and hasidic leader, the Master of Gur, failed to lift his colleague's depression through encouragement, support, and intellectual stimulation. One day, upon hearing about Rabbi Soloveitchik's deteriorating mental and physical condition, Rabbi Meir Simha Ha'Kohen, a brilliant scholar and student of Rabbi Soloveitchik, hurried to visit his teacher. Rabbi Meir attempted unsuccessfully to engage his rabbi in a talmudic discussion, as the latter was totally engulfed by worry for his beloved colleague. At one point, Rabbi Meir quoted some of the Torah novella that he had heard from Rabbi Diskin when he had visited him in jail some months previously. As Rabbi Meir discerned some reaction from his teacher, he began to challenge and criticize Rabbi Diskin's new insights and interpretations on certain talmudic topics and vigorously disputed the conclusions. Upon hearing criticism of his beloved teacher, Rabbi Soloveitchik began to defend him by quoting texts and rabbinical authorities and explaining and analyzing his teacher's Torah. Instead of remitting, Rabbi Meir continued to challenge Rabbi Diskin's Torah, which prompted Rabbi Soloveitchik to raise his voice and marshal all his brilliance, analytic skills, and energy to refute his student's arguments and prove that his mentor was correct. Rabbi Meir soon began to raise other talmudic topics to which Rabbi Soloveitchik also responded in an increasingly intense manner.

After concluding their talmudic deliberations, Rabbi Soloveitchik accompanied his visitor to the synagogue, where he had not gone for a long time. Shortly afterward, Rabbi Soloveitchik resumed his teaching and regular activities as the spiritual leader of his community.

Another example of a creative manipulative intervention on the part of a respected rabbinic figure is an incident related about Rabbi Mordechai Lebton, the Chief Rabbi and head of the rabbinical court in Syria in the nineteenth century. One day a distraught couple appeared before the rabbi for a divorce. Though the couple had been happily married for many years, during the last year the husband had become depressed, angry, and impatient with his wife because she was barren and therefore decided to divorce her. The rabbi unsuccessfully attempted to persuade the husband to reconsider his decision since his wife was a fine meritorious person.

The rabbi, a highly intelligent and perceptive person who was able to penetrate the inner recesses of people and discern their dynamics and weaknesses, decided on a plan of action to cause the husband to revive his affection and appreciation of his wife. He instructed the couple to return the following day for the purpose of arranging the divorce procedures.

The next day, as the rabbi was preparing to divorce the couple, his student (upon pre-arranged instructions) barged in and whispered into the rabbi's ear.

The rabbi unexpectedly began scolding and yelling at his student to the astonishment of the estranged couple. When queried about his unusual behavior, the rabbi explained that his student had crossed the line of propriety. "My student had the audacity to ask me to hasten the divorce proceedings so that he could propose marriage to this wonderful woman."

Upon hearing this, the shocked husband informed the rabbi that he decided to return to his wife and asked the rabbi for his blessing. The following year, a son was born to the happy couple.

The "Hafetz Haim" was consulted about how to help a young scholar, who had a fine personality, came from a good family, but was of short stature, which made it difficult to find him a suitable wife. The rabbi advised that he should wear elevated shoes at the first meeting in order to give him a taller appearance but not afterwards. The explanation given was that the potential mates should not be repelled and discouraged on first sight and that after getting to know him, his physical stature would not be a significant decisive factor.

It appears that the rabbinic attitude regarding the ends justifying the means is quite flexible, as they sanction and use manipulation when noble goals are involved such as the enhancement of people's emotional and social well-being.

NOTES

1. JE Brown and PT Slee, "Paradoxical strategies: The ethics of intervention." *Professional Psychology: Research and Practice*, 17, no. 6, (1986): 487–489.

2. J Haley, *Problem-solving Therapy*. (San-Francisco, Jossey-Bass, 1976).

3. A Frances, J Clarkin and S Perry, *Differential Therapeutics in Psychiatry: The Art and Science of Treatment Selection*. (Brunner/Mazel, New York, 1984).

4. J Haley, *Uncommon Therapy: The Psychiatric Techniques of Milton Erickson, M.D.* (New York, W.W. Norton, 1973).

5. C Karlinsky, *The First of the Brisk Dynasty* (Jerusalem: Jerusalem Institute, 1984). (in Hebrew).

Part Two

PSYCHOTHERAPY AND JUDAISM

Chapter Seven

Is Psychotherapy Possible with Unbelievers?—The Care of the Ultra-Orthodox Community

David Greenberg, M.D., MRC Psych.

INTRODUCTION

This presentation will address the issues involved in developing a psychotherapy service for a particular population in Israeli society: the ultra-orthodox (haredim).[1] This community is "characterized by a distinctive garb and physical appearance that includes long black coats, large black hats, and full beards . . . social interaction with outsiders is minimal . . . rigid adherence to the laws of the Torah" (page 53,[2]). They constitute over 50% of the population of the catchment area of North Jerusalem,[1] served by the Community Mental Health Center of the Herzog Hospital. Because of this large populace, this issue is of practical importance.

There is a theoretical issue involved, however, in every way as important as the above practical one, for the issue involves the meeting of two cultures: the "psychotherapy" culture[3] and a minority cultural group. Defining the issues and attempting to find solutions is relevant wherever such an encounter occurs, be it in Israel with new Soviet and Ethiopian immigrants, or in any country with Community Mental Health services attempting to reach out to minorities.[4]

The facts are sobering. Studies in the United States[5,6] and the United Kingdom[7] have pointed out that minority groups do not tend to seek help from the Community Mental Health services of the main culture. When they do, they have a higher drop-out rate.

Furthermore, the therapist appears to have difficulty receiving these referrals, for patients from minority groups have a far higher chance of being offered medication or ECT[8], and a lower chance of being offered psychotherapy.[9] The few minority patients who do return a second time for help should not expect that anyone will speak to them!

A similar pattern of the utilization of services is found among ultra-orthodox referrals to Community Mental Health Centers (CMHC) in Israel. Twenty-five percent of clinic referrals in North Jerusalem are ultra-orthodox (haredim),[10] while they constitute 50% of the community. These figures mean that the non-ultra-orthodox are three times more likely to seek public psychiatric help than are the ultra-orthodox. Furthermore, diagnoses of schizophrenia and major or depressive disorder with psychotic features are far more common among the ultra-orthodox, while anxiety-related and adjustment disorders are more common among the non-ultra-orthodox referrals.

In conclusion, the ultra-orthodox are underrepresented among new referrals to CMHCs, are more likely to drop out, and tend to present more severe psychopathology. Clearly, a significant proportion of the community is failing to use the available facilities. Why? What can we do about it?

The problem may be usefully divided into five components: 1) The setting; 2) The patient; 3) The therapist; 4) The therapeutic alliance; 5) The therapeutic options (discussed in the concluding section).

THE SETTING

Every year, over 1% of the local population of north Jerusalem visits the CMHC, although the morbidity rate in the community is much higher (to 15%).[11] Everyone thinks twice before seeking psychiatric help, both because it means acknowledging a psychiatric problem in oneself, and because it means possibly being seen entering a psychiatric establishment. Stigma is a powerful social force and even more so in ultra-orthodox society. In a society where the introduction of couples is arranged, and family pedigrees are checked, a history of mental illness is a major blot on that pedigree. Families will try to hide the problem, or seek private help rather than be seen in a public clinic. One family member with a psychiatric record affects the marriage prospects of everyone else.

A second issue involves the fact that the clinic is a component of secular Israeli society. The ultra-orthodox are not just distinguished by their religious beliefs, or by their outward appearance. Their culture also has particular economic, social and political aspects. In Israel, more than in other countries with ultra-orthodox communities, the surrounding culture, possibly because it is also Jewish, is seen as unacceptable. Thus, separate existence is a virtue. Men often study and do not work all their lives, nor in general do they serve in the army. Schooling is separate and no ultra-orthodox attend university. The ultra-orthodox live in separate enclaves, and may even use separate health services. As for psychiatric problems, "briyut nefesh" is the Hebrew term for psychiatry, where "nefesh" (soul), is a biblical word with Kabbalistic ramifications. How can non-religious therapists using secular knowledge possibly understand the Jewish soul? For reasons both political and social, let alone religious, the CMHC is avoided.

Now let us enter the CMHC building. Few or none of the staff are ultra-orthodox; the women may be wearing trousers and married women may have uncovered hair. Being asked to sit in a room with a therapist of the opposite sex creates the problem of "yihud". All these problems arise before the therapist and patient have even said hello.

THE PATIENT

Before discussing ultra-orthodox patients, a general problem with most patients is that they don't perceive things "correctly". They invariably complain of pain, and blame others as sources of upset in their lives and their general unhappiness. Furthermore, they misunderstand the role of the therapists. They expect to be told what is wrong with them or their situation and what they should do about it. Therapists then have to teach patients that it is the patient who must discover what his real underlying problems are and that it is the patient who must discover the solutions, (When the patient then fails to keep his second appointment, his action is called passive-aggressive behavior).

Most patients then have different expectations from therapists, and it is hardly surprising that only the elite, the "psychologically-minded", enter psychotherapy.[12]

If we now turn to the ultra-orthodox, what do they do if they have a problem in everyday life? They approach their rabbi or teacher, irrespective of whether the problem is religious, ethical or personal. He is asked a question, a "she'ela", and responds with an answer, a "teshuva". The problem is posed as a question, the solution as a series of instructions. By viewing the norms of a society, we discover their expectations. There is, therefore, a marked gap between the expectations of the ultra-orthodox patient and the mental health therapist.

The ultra-orthodox patient has spent his life studying religious texts that also include "mussar" that heal disturbances of the soul. His sources of knowledge may be unknown to the therapist, yet the latter is expected to help him. The rabbi's "teshuva" is couched in quotations from earlier Rabbis, yet the therapist knows none of these sources. How can a person ignorant of these sources help the patient? The patient feels suspicious and uncomfortable, creating an atmosphere that is not the ideal basis for successful therapy.

Furthermore, the patient feels ashamed and a failure. He questions himself, that if the texts are meant to mend one's soul, to heal sorrow, then why is he coming for help? Is he of weak faith? This dilemma is not unique to this group, and has been well described by Koltko, concerning Mormons.[13]

THE THERAPIST

Living in the cultural and political reality of Israel, the therapist is beset by a series of problems; the distinctive features of any minority culture are usually perceived by the majority culture as inferior, and their social relations are perceived as shallow. The fact that most ultra-orthodox (haredim) do not serve in the army, especially the fighting battalions, can create very antagonistic feelings in the therapist. The therapist thinks: "I risk my life, my children risk theirs, and we protect you!" This is a conscious or unconscious thought that creates a tense atmosphere for therapy. Consider the following encounter:

An ultra-orthodox man has asked the receptionist if he can speak to the clinic director. He takes out a religious text that deals with religious problems in medical treatment and shows the director a statement that any religious person coming for psychological help should be sure to go only to a God-fearing therapist. He asks to be seen by such a religious person. The director then replies curtly, "If you wish to be seen by a religious therapist, I suggest you encourage your children to go to University, complete a training in medicine and psychiatry, and then we will employ them in our clinic. Until that starts to happen, there will be no ultra-orthodox therapists."[14]

The underlying issue involves the racist attitudes held by most therapists encountering minority patients, be it White treating Black, Israeli treating Arab, or Secular treating Ultra-Orthodox. Gorkin[15] has noted several typical ways that a therapist may react to minority patients. He may show an exaggerated interest in the patient's cultural aspects, losing sight of the patient's personal problems, or he may behave as though therapy is a haven from prejudice, from which he, the therapist, is totally free, or he may be aggressive, viewing the patient's culture as inferior. If the patient is newly-religious, thrilled by his revelations of a life of belief, the therapist may also feel envy at the confidence and enthusiasm he sees.[16]

THE THERAPEUTIC ALLIANCE

The initial contact between the patient and the therapist is of vital importance and contains various factors. Usually, when a patient first comes for help, the therapist asks the accompanying family or friends to wait outside and speaks alone with the patient in order to get to know him. Very often our ultra-orthodox patients are accompanied by their rabbi/teacher. Not only does the Rabbi not leave, but often places his seat between the patient and the therapist. Does one ask him to leave?

From the outset, the patient has been feeling suspicious and uncomfortable. His teacher may well have brought him to the clinic and thus sees himself as responsible for the patient's welfare. From our experience, the therapist should allow himself to be the minority in the room. As will be noted later, it was only during discussions with religious leaders that the author understood the interpositioning pose taken by the teacher—the person being interviewed is the therapist. The object of the interview is two fold, for it involves the therapist's assessment of the patient and also the teacher's assessment of the therapist.

Other issues in the patient/therapist interaction can arise. Patient and therapist, from different cultures, therefore have different communication styles. For example, different cultures may maintain different interpersonal distances (a science known as proxemics). If the ultra-orthodox patient comes up close to the therapist, too close for the therapist's comfort, the therapist may involuntarily withdraw to a further distance, and the patient may well sense this as rejection. These impressions are also immediately conveyed to the patient by the distances between the chairs in the interviewing room.[17]

Body movement and facial expression, known as kinesics, also vary between cultures. Western psychiatrists are usually aware of eye contact, and many ultra-orthodox referrals are brought in with their heads down, eyes to the floor. Until it is known how the average ultra-orthodox community member relates to strangers and to strange situations, therapists should be wary of making conclusions, and should also not feel excluded when greeted in this way.[18]

Language is also a barrier, for every community has its own vocabulary. Western patients will describe themselves as depressed or sad, while the ultra-orthodox either speak of "fears", having a variety of meanings, or of "mara shchora", meaning literally melancholy (black bile). These feelings are barriers to forming a therapeutic alliance. Our incomprehension or irritation can also be felt, and everyone, both patient and therapist, retreats to their corner.

Sue[19] has analyzed the therapeutic alliance in the cross cultural patient-therapist interaction and has concluded that there are two main factors involved: credibility of the therapist in the eyes of the patient, and the ability of the therapist to "give" something early on in his contact with the patient.

Credibility is a universal factor in creating a therapeutic alliance. If you are told that you must see a specialist, your first thought is, "Who is recommended?" We all want to see someone who is "good", i.e. who has credibility. This factor, however, is more critical when a patient comes from a minority culture uneasy in its contacts with the majority culture. It is even more critical and becomes a greater problem in the ultra-orthodox community, as the medical profession has dubious credibility, e.g. "The best of doctors go to hell".[20] Even more damning is the attitude to seeing doctors amongst the fringe sect of Bratslav Hasidim, following the words of their leader, Rabbi Nachman of Bratslav, who said, "The Angel of Death cannot do all the killings himself, so he appoints agents in each locality. These agents are the physicians."[21]

How does one "give" something to the patient? This can include reassurance, normalization ("Many go through what you are going through"), clarification of the problems, skills acquisition, goal setting and anxiety relief. Attention to this detail of "giving", during the first contact with the patient, increases the therapist's credibility and discourages dropout.

The discussion of these issues has been presented in a variety of cross-cultural situations, in reviews by psychiatrists, having varying degrees of clinical experience and knowledge of anthropology.[9,19,22,23,24]

Is there not one important ingredient missing? What is the view of the consumer? What does the ultra-orthodox community think of the Community Mental Health services? For the purpose of this presentation, two ultra-orthodox rabbis were interviewed, selected because they are leaders who deal with young men with psychiatric problems and they have extensive contact with the CMHCs. It was considered that the opinions of users would possibly be too individual, affected by their personal experience, while the opinions of the rabbis were of interest for two reasons. First, because of the structure of their society, most people will turn to these figures in order to discuss their problems and in order to decide whether to seek professional help. Second, their opinions are an overview based on a wide variety of cases and subsequent contact with the CMHCs. It was clear, however, that the rabbis had different opinions on certain topics, reflecting their personal approaches, the populations they dealt with, and the subgroup of ultra-orthodoxy they belonged to.

The first question concerned their criteria for deciding whether someone was a case for treatment. The answers reflected the close social structure. Everyone is a member of certain systems: Family, yeshiva, synagogue, Hasidic group. The main definition of disorder in community members is that they do not fit into their system. The leaders of that system, the Rebbe, Rosh Yeshiva or father discuss the problem at first. If, for example, the suggested solutions are unsuccessful in the Yeshiva, then the family will become involved. Only if no advances are made, will professional advice then be sought.

At this stage, the rabbi or teacher prefers to consult the professional in the absence of the patient, describing the case and asking for advice. Only if the professional considers the case to be complicated or an interview to be necessary, does the teacher then bring the patient. The teacher, however, still thinks: "He's still not out of my hands. We will go for counseling and the professional may then suggest medication or some other direction that I haven't thought of, such as sport, work or a period off from study."

It is at this point in our discussion, that we should recall the three-way. interview and the "intrusive" position taken by the teacher. His intention is to be the go-between, between the professional and the patient, who is still "in his hands." If someone suffers internally, with nothing noticeable in his external social performance, he may seek help from an individual from within the community—but he is not a psychiatric "case" in the eyes of the community.

The second question involves the fact that ultra-orthodox cases of depression are rarely seen in the CMHCs. How does the community handle them? Interestingly, the rabbis who were interviewed both distinguished between what have been called exogenous and endogenous depression. For example, boys in Yeshiva often find it hard to keep up with their learning and become despairing before examinations or may become envious when their fellow students marry, while they remain single. Such cases need spiritual encouragement (as will be discussed in the next question) and a change of environment: less pressure on studies, encouragement to go on outings. Such cases are therefore not brought for professional help. Patients experiencing depression with no external cause are brought for medication, which "gets them out of it and they get better."

The third question approaches the subject of psychotherapy. What do you offer people at a time of crisis? When do you bring them for talking therapy?

In this case, both rabbis largely concurred, similar themes recurring in their responses. Said one, "We treat such problems in the community; we give him a boost with talk of belief and trust in G-d, that he must not despair, at the same time encouraging him to discuss the situation. We tell him to strengthen his Faith, that everything is from Heaven, that no man moves a finger on Earth unless guided by G-d. We tell him that the world is a very narrow bridge not just for him, and that he should cry to G-d. We remind him of the privilege of being a Jew keeping the Torah. We encourage him to listen to soothing Niggunim (the tunes sung by Chassidic leaders), to read stories of miracles from the lives of the great Rabbis, and to learn Aggada (stories from the Talmud) rather than the more academic sections." Psychiatrists are only used for prescribing medication, as one of the rabbis explained, "We don't know what outlook on life the patient will hear from a psychologist. It can harm a boy. It is a different outlook on life. I don't know what sort of "epikores" I'll find. (An epikores is someone who rejects the existence of God and the practice of religious law). He'll have no belief in God, and will say that everything is due to nature; tell the boy to be more free, encourage him to eat more, go to the seaside, meet girls, in short: enjoy life. But our outlook on life is based on faith."

The other rabbi said simply, "We very very rarely involve psychologists. A psychiatrist can be like a physician, treating an infection, while a psychologist may interfere on matters of basic communal values."

The final question concerns what the requirements are of a therapist. While one rabbi sought a "God-fearing man", the other stated clearly that he need not be religious. The second said, "What matters is that he understands the religious way of life and respects each person with their outlook." He went on to tell of a rabbi-cum-psychologist, very popular in some circles, whose advice to a young student so appalled him that he took counsel from a leader of the community, who described the advice as "the counsel of Ahitophel", and told him to avoid referring students to the therapist. Furthermore, some religious therapists are nevertheless anti-ultra-orthodox, being particularly antagonistic towards the Yeshiva lifestyle.

Other questions on the reasons for women being referred so rarely, and the misgivings regarding psychiatric hospital facilities were discussed with the two rabbis and will be presented elsewhere.

CONCLUSIONS

1. The ultra-orthodox society is highly structured. It is vital that Community Mental Health services respect that structure and work within it. Just as community care in other communities involves regular contact with family practitioners, community care with the ultra-orthodox should begin with regular contact with religious leaders.
2. As a consequence, communal leaders will get to know individual mental health workers, and will come to respect their professional opinions. In this way, the professionals will gain credibility within the ultra-orthodox community.
3. Therapists involved in this work require regular supervision, including discussion of their attitudes and feelings toward the group. Knowledge about the ultra-orthodox way of life is necessary, although knowledge alone is inadequate, and has been described as "distal", meaning that knowledge alone will not produce good therapy, even leading insensi-

tive therapists to treat all their ultra-orthodox patients in the same way.[19]

4. Therapists who work in this area should, if possible, speak Yiddish and should have a basic religious knowledge. Testing of the intelligence and orientation of ultra-orthodox patients should focus on blessings, religious festivals, and the weekly Torah reading. Asking the name of the Prime Minister or the site of the Peace conference are topics that not only emphasize patient-therapist. differences, but leave the patient feeling suspicious or disapproving of the therapist.

5. As we have discussed elsewhere, specific knowledge of the characteristic behaviors of subgroups is necessary. For Bratslav Hasidim, for example, nocturnal visits to the fields and tearful prayers at the tombs of the righteous are normative behaviors. Mistakes will be few, however, if regular contact with the teacher is maintained.[25]

6. The therapists should continue working with teachers and rabbis throughout the patient's therapy, particularly deferring any religious questions to them. Described by Westermeyer as "culture brokers", these intermediaries are not only there to protect the patient, but may also be the therapist's advocate.[26] If cognitive or behavioral therapy is offered, the teacher should be used as a co-therapist.

7. An optimal system may be to discuss the findings and treatment options with the patient and his teacher following the completion of the assessment, with attention to "giving" some relief or guidance at the first contact.

8. It is not that a particular therapy per se is non-kosher. It is the therapist whose credibility is in question.

9. Therapists should be wary of offering a standard "ultra-Orthodox treatment package". Assessment and suggestions for the appropriate treatment with a full description and explanation are necessary in each case. The teacher/rabbi can then decide with the patient whether to continue therapy or not.

10. All forms of therapy have been used with the ultra-orthodox community, such as: a cognitive therapy text with an introduction of approval by leading rabbis, and a collection of supportive quotes from religious sources;[27] behavior therapy with limits set by rabbis,[28] and a form of behavior therapy described by an eminent rabbi in a book of responsa, with a chapter on psychological disturbances.[29] Dynamic psychotherapy has been most distrusted,[30] yet has also been carefully evaluated[22]. Religious belief should only be discussed if seen to be serving neurotic functions, although this may best be discussed first in a three-way meeting with the

teacher, when it is made clear that there exists also non-neurotic religious belief.

ACKNOWLEDGEMENT

The author would like to thank Eli Witztum whose energy and interest stimulated many of the ideas in this article.

NOTES

1. I Shilhav and M Friedman, *Growth and Segregation—the Ultra-orthodox Community of Jerusalem*. (Jerusalem: Jerusalem Institute for Israel Studies, 1985).

2. WB Helmreich, *The World of the Yeshiva: An Intimate Portrait of Orthodox Jewry*. (New Haven: Yale University, 1982).

3. AE Ivey, "Counseling and psychotherapy: Toward a new perspective." In *Cross cultural Counseling and Psychotherapy* eds AJ Marsella and PB Pederson (Elmsford NY: Pergamon, 1981).

4. S Acharyya, S Moorhouse, J Kareem and R Littlewood, "Nafsiyat: A psychotherapy center for ethnic minorities." *Psychiatric Bulletin of the Royal College of Psychiatrists* 13, (1989): 358–60.

5. S Sue, "Community mental health services to minority groups: Some optimism, some pessimism." *American Psychologist*, 32, (1977): 616–24.

6. RL Hough, JA Landsverk, M Kamo, A Burnam, DM Timbers, II Escobar and DA Regier, "Utilization of health and mental health services by Los Angeles Mexican Americans and non-Hispanic whites." *Archives of General Psychiatry* 44, (1987): 702–09.

7. B Ineichen, "The mental health of Asians in Britain: Little disease or underreporting?" *British Medical Journal*, 300, (1990): 1669–70.

8. BI Good and MJ DelVecchio Good, "The cultural context of diagnosis and therapy: A view from medical anthropology." in *Medical Health Research and Practice in Minority Communities: Development of Culturally Sensitive Training Programs*. eds M Miranda and H. Kitano, (Washington DC: United States Government Printing Office for NIMH, 1986), 1–27.

9. R Littlewood and S Cross, "Ethnic minorities and psychiatric services." *Sociology of Health and Illness* 2, (1980): 194–201.

10. JT Buchbinder, unpublished data.

11. LN Robins, JE Helzer, MM Weissman, H Orvaschel, E Gruenberg, JD Burke and DA Regier, "Lifetime prevalence of specific psychiatric disorders in three sites." *Archives of General Psychiatry*, 41, (1984): 949–58.

12. J Wohl, "Integration of cultural awareness into psychotherapy." *American Journal of Psychotherapy* 43, (1989): 343–55.

13. ME Koltko, "How religious beliefs affect psychotherapy: The example of Mormonism." *Psychotherapy* 27, (1990): 132–41.

14. D Greenberg and E Witztum, "Problems in the treatment of religious patients." *American Journal of Psychotherapy* 45, (October 1991).

15. M Gorkin, *The Use of Countertransference*. (Northvale NJ: Jason Aronson, 1987).

16. MH Spero and R Mester, "Countenransference envy toward the religious patient." *American Journal of Psychoanalysis* 48, (1988): 43–55.

17. JV Jensen, "Perspective on nonverbal intercultural communication." in *Intercultural Communication: A Reader.* eds. LA Samovar and RE Porter, (Belmont CA: Wadsworth, 1985).

18. DW Sue, "Culture-specific strategies in counseling: A conceptual framework." *Professional Psychology: Research and Practice* 2, (1990): 424–33.

19. S Sue and N Zane, "The role of culture and cultural techniques in psychotherapy." *American Psychologist* 42, (1987): 37–45.

20. Mishna, Mo'ed.

21. A Kaplan, *Rabbi Nachman's Wisdom*. (New York: Bratslav, 1972).

22. MH Spero, (ed). *Psychotherapy of the Religious Patient*. (Springfield Ill: Thomas, 1985).

23. R Littlewood and M Lipsedge, *Aliens and Alienists*, 2nd ed. (London: Unwin Hyman, 1989).

24. AM Jackson, "Evolution of ethnocultural psychotherapy." *Psychotherapy* 27, (1990): 428–35.

25. E Witztum, D Greenberg and JT Buchbinder, ""A very narrow bridge": Diagnosis and management of mental illness among Bratslav Hasidim." *Psychotherapy*, 27, (1990): 124–31.

26. J Westenneyer, "Cultural factors in clinical assessment." *Journal of Consulting and Clinical Psychology*, 55, (1987): 471–78.

27. Z Pliskin, *Gateway to Happiness*. (Jerusalem: Aish Ha Torah, 1983).

28. D Greenberg, "The behavioral treatment of religious compulsions." *Journal of Psychology and Judaism,* 11, (1987): 41–47.

29. Y Kanievski, *Kraina De'Agarta (The reader of the letter)*. (Bnei Brak, 1986).

30. A Amsel, *Judaism and Psychology*, (New York: Feldheim, 1969).

Chapter Eight

Initial Religious Counseling for a Male Orthodox Adolescent Homosexual

Joel B. Wolowelsky, Ph.D. and
Bernard L. Weinstein, M.D.

We present here a discussion of possible reactions by a rabbi, religious counselor or teacher to a male orthodox adolescent who seeks advice and counseling because he feels he is a homosexual. It is not our intention to propose a full program for halakhically-valid psychological therapy for homosexuals, or even to enter into the debate on whether every homosexual can be helped to change his sexual orientation. Indeed, the latter debate is confused by the fact that many homosexuals who appear incapable of changing their orientation might in fact be individuals who bolted treatment when insight became too painful, who were misaligned with their particular therapist, or who would have changed had their homosexuality caused them sufficient psychological pain and anguish.[1]

Admittedly, a rabbi or religious counselor might not be trained to complete such psychological counseling, and the proper approach might well be to refer the adolescent to a competent therapist. However, the initial encounter with a religious authority figure may well influence any possible future counseling and therefore demands a thoughtful, responsible reaction.

It should not be necessary to belabor the point that some responses would be counterproductive. Of course, the counselor must adhere to the halakhic position that homosexual acts are absolutely incompatible with a Torah perspective. Nonetheless, reiterating this position at this time is not necessarily productive. It simply restates something already known to the adolescent, who after all, is seeking not a permissive ruling for homosexuality but aid in grappling with what he perceives to be an irresistible urge to act against his halakhic commitment. Simply telling him that he may not violate halakha may frighten him into believing that there is no help available. At the very least, he deserves praise for his courage in coming forward to confront the problem.

Even when it is obvious that the teenager must be referred to another counselor, it is important in the initial encounter to invest time in a positive discussion. If the adolescent gets the message that the rabbi/ teacher is frightened or not competent to cope with the issue, he might fear that there is no solution to his problem. Of course, an adult aware of his own incompetence to confront an issue must not attempt to deal with the adolescent himself (and must know to whom he can direct a student). But the referral must be done in a way that is reassuring and not intimidating.

Religious counselors and professional therapists have very different yet legitimate agendas in their respective discussions with homosexuals. The latter's job is to help the individual come to terms with himself by resolving his underlying conflicts, helping him become as autonomously productive as possible. Religious counselors, on the other hand, have an obligation to help the individual grow in his religious conviction and observance. These objectives are not inherently contradictory, but they should be understood and sorted out.

In order to avoid the contradiction they perceive between their professional and halakhic commitments, some halakhically-committed psychodynamically-oriented therapists paradoxically refer homosexual clients to other therapists who, they believe, maintain a value-free attitude towards homosexuality. Needless to say, we reject out of hand the notion that religious therapists are incapable of helping people with a homosexual orientation, although reconciling this perceived contradiction is beyond the scope of this paper.

A crucial task of the religious counselor in the initial conference is to assess any immediate danger to the student and assure a positive atmosphere and framework for future discussions. The counselor must be aware of the danger of suicidal thoughts and directly, though delicately, raise the question of how tortured the student might be by his homosexual thoughts. The student himself might raise the question of intense pain or depression, and it is reasonable to ask if he has ever considered hurting himself. A positive response should be met calmly but not dismissed. The counselor should ask if any specific plan of action has been considered or if the adolescent has in any way (recently or in the past) already attempted to harm himself. Generally speaking, the more concrete the plans are for a suicide, the more likely it is to be actualized. It is also useful to ask if there is a family history of suicide, depression, or other severe psychiatric illness.

Suicidal thoughts need immediate attention by a trained professional, and the rabbi or counselor is usually not trained to address this very real danger to the adolescent. Indeed, if suicidal ideation is present, it is probably necessary to address the depression professionally before dealing with the homosexuality. Thus, when suggesting a referral to a teenager (and, later, to him and his parents together), the point should be made that while the whole homosexuality issue may well ultimately reflect a central organizing conflict in the adolescent's life, it might, on the other hand, represent merely one of several contributing factors to the suicidal depressive state being presented.

The religious counselor should address the sense of guilt and feelings of insanity that such a young man might often be feeling. Guilt has already impelled the individual to seek help; at this point it can be paralyzing rather than positive. To some extent, psychological pain and anguish is necessary to motivate a successful therapeutic experience. But an overly tortured, frightened person can hardly address underlying conflicts. The individual must be calmed and given enough confidence to find the strength to effectively grapple with his problems.

A forthright statement should be made that despite the fact that homosexual acts are prohibited by the Torah, homosexual thoughts do not necessarily reflect being "crazy." From a Torah perspective the young man, notwithstanding his homosexual thoughts, is probably quite sane.

To better understand this last point, it might be helpful to consider that there is no specific halakhic proscription against eating feces. This is no accident, because healthy people naturally eschew eating excrement, and we would quite naturally question the mental health of people who enjoy eating it. If normal people would not consider doing something, the Torah has no need to prohibit it.

But the Torah does prohibit eating unkosher food, and even kosher food must be avoided if it is medically harmful. Yet neither a healthy person who eats pork nor an individual with a heart condition who eats cholesterol-rich food is *ipso facto* crazy. With regard to the former, *Sifra* (*Kedoshim*, end of *perek* 9) presents a position later adopted by Rambam (*Shemone Perakim* VI): "Do not say, 'I do not want to eat meat together with milk; I do not want to wear clothes made of *shatnez* (a mixture of linen and wool); I do not want to enter into a prohibited sexual relationship.' Rather, he should say 'I do indeed want to do it, yet I will not, for my Father in Heaven has forbidden it.'" And while we might feel that the cardiac patient who chooses to eat red meat is irresponsible, we intuitively know the difference between stupidity and insanity.

On the other hand, overweight people who are trying desperately to address their heart condition by losing weight and yet cannot control their compulsion to overeat are, indeed, ill. What Rabbi Joseph B. Soloveitchik maintains in theory regarding man's emotional life when confronting the death of a relative has a broader validity: The halakha was firmly convinced that man is free and that he is master not only of his deeds but over his emotions as well. The halakha held the view that man's mastery over his emotional life is unqualified and that he is capable of changing thought patterns, emotional structures and experimental motifs.[2]

Whatever the extent to which this theoretical framework is true of a specific individual, it is nonetheless true that it is the compulsion, the absence of free will, which is the illness, not the sense that the unhealthy food would taste delicious.

With regard to heterosexual desire, we certainly regard the sex drive as normal and healthy. We expect healthy people to be able to overcome that drive when sex is halakhically prohibited. Indeed, Rabbi Joseph B. Soloveitchik sees the ability to overcome such desires as the hallmark of human dignity: Bride and groom are young, physically strong and passionately in love with each other. Both have patiently waited for this rendezvous to take place. Just one more step and their love would have been fulfilled, a vision realized. Suddenly the bride and groom make a movement of recoil. He, gallantly, like a chivalrous knight, exhibits paradoxical heroism. He takes his own defeat. There is no glamour attached to his withdrawal. The latter is not a spectacular gesture, since there are no witnesses to admire and laud him. The heroic act did not take place in the presence of jubilating crowds.

This kind of divine dialectical discipline is not limited to man's sexual life, but extends to all areas of natural drive and temptation. The hungry person must forgo the pleasure of taking food, no matter how strong the temptation; men of property must forgo the pleasure of acquisition, if the latter is halachically and morally wrong. In a word, Halacha requires of man that he possess the capability of withdrawal.[3]

Halakha focuses on the ability to withdraw from executing a natural impulse, not from feeling the impulse itself. A young man who has homosexual thoughts but who can control his actions is not ill. But a person who has an irresistible compulsion to act against his values does need psychological help irrespective of the nature of the compulsion. Thus, even in cases where homosexual desire is long-standing and defines a deep and apparently unalterable aspect of the personality, halakha calls us to the heroic act of renunciation.

It is interesting to speculate why the Torah stresses that homosexual acts are an "abomination" (Lev. 18:22; 20:13) along with the other prohibited abominable sexual acts (Lev. 18:26–29), just as it labels unkosher food "abominations" (Deut. 14:3). But that is neither here nor there. The Torah forbids these because they are quite normal but—in the Torah's view—improper. Sometimes we can understand the reason for a prohibition; indeed, the argument against homosexuality is as cogent as that in support of kashrut. But whether or not we understand the rationale of a specific prohibition, we can assume that any Torah prohibition implies that it is something which is part of the common human situation that is being prohibited.

Thus we need not even argue against the psychological position that holds that many healthy people have homosexual thoughts at one time or another. The Torah's position is that the normal quality of any impulse is irrelevant to its ethical or halakhic character. Homosexuality and seafood are abominations and hence forbidden because the Torah says so; the Torah does not necessarily forbid them because they are by their nature—like feces- repulsive.

This position is reassuring for the religious adolescent plagued by homosexual thoughts. If he is crazy, there may be no hope. If he is basically normal—struggling in this area as all people do in one area or another—then there may well be a chance for him to lead a rich, halakhically valid life. Halakha's opposition to the pro-homosexuality campaign being waged in our secular society does not target the claim that homosexual impulses are normal. On the other hand, halakha's position is that the normalcy of an impulse is not its license. On the contrary, the ability to retreat from one's natural impulses is at times the hallmark of mental health and halakhically ethical conduct. Thus, halakha rejects the current proposition that sexual fulfillment is the *summum bonum* of life, arguing that a halakhically ethical life often denies the heterosexual as well as the homosexual the possibility of total sexual fulfillment.

Somewhere during the counseling session, the adolescent should be asked if it is all right to put a number of straightforward questions on the table. It is not necessary to deal with them all at this meeting, but touching on them will help create a framework for future discussions, whether with the religious counselor or the therapist. The counselor's ability to hear all this information without responding negatively sets the tone for all future discussions. No matter what is said, the adolescent must have continual and convincing reassurance that he still remains a person worthy of love and understanding. If the rabbi or counselor responds with shock, revulsion, or damnation to what he hears, the young man might lose the confidence required to confront and solve his problem—or at least lose the trust necessary to ever discuss the issue again with a religious authority figure. One need not fear that lack of reprimand will be taken as license. It is enough to state once at the end that specific items mentioned might be halakhically prohibited but the problem as a whole can be dealt with.

It is worth mentioning a few specific questions that might be explored in the initial counseling session, even before referral is made to an outside therapist. First and foremost is the question of whether the adolescent has reached his conclusion regarding his sexual orientation on the basis of his thoughts or his actions?

Adolescents can misinterpret homosexual thoughts as signs of a permanent orientation. Homosexual thoughts might be motivated by the general sexual confusion common to many adolescents, an attempt to interpret public discussions about homosexuality that are unintelligible to the teenager, or "replaying" a shocking scene to which the young person had been exposed. Such thoughts can be frightening, causing the adolescent to fixate on them. The counselor should ask the student to relate some of their details. Even if there is a serious underlying problem that must be further addressed in therapy, showing him that these frightening thoughts can be openly discussed in a nonjudgmental manner with a religious authority figure creates a healthy atmosphere for future discussions. If the adolescent is having frequent sexual thoughts, it is pointless to say things like, "Put such thoughts out of your head." If he were able to, he would not be speaking to the counselor at all.

It is true that there is a prohibition of *hirhur* [fantasizing] about illicit sexual acts and that to some extent this may apply to relating them in a conversation. But the religious counselor may develop an inaccurate picture of the reality being described by the adolescent if only generalities are used, making him less able to offer concrete and reassuring advice. Moreover, the teenager might misinterpret the counselor's reluctance to listen to his fantasies as either a suggestion that the situation is too hopeless to deal with or that he should not trust the therapist to whom he is being referred.

Sometimes a teenager assumes he is a homosexual simply because he is not part of the carefree and promiscuous heterosexual sexual scene popularized on television. Too scared to discuss the issue with anyone, he never hears the reassurance that shyness and reserve is completely normal. An open, reassuring conversation that communicates that it is the promiscuous scene which is unhealthy and immoral can often relieve much of the adolescent's anxiety.

Even actual homosexual acts themselves are not necessarily an indication of homosexuality. Though clearly prohibited by halakha, some homosexual experimentation may emerge at camp or in a yeshiva dorm. The widespread campaign to accept the unalterability of a homosexual orientation compounds the teenager's normal difficulty to see the many possibilities available in any situation. Unable to discuss these activities with an adult, he may well have convinced himself that he is a homosexual. A calm, nonjudgmental, open discussion with a religious authority can give the young man an opportunity to come to terms with these past actions and move on to a healthy, productive life.

It was not our intention to present here the details of a halakhically-valid therapeutic strategy for dealing with students troubled by homosexual thoughts. It is not the duty of the religious counselor to have worked out a thorough therapeutic approach to properly address a student who approaches him for guidance in this issue. Rather, he must be prepared to calm the student, offer him reassurance and make a proper referral to a halakhically-sensitive fully-trained therapist.

The omission of three items of general rabbinic counseling from our "Initial religious Counseling for Male Orthodox Adolescent Homosexuals" might have created the mistaken impression that they do not apply in the emotionally-charged context. We would therefore take this opportunity to briefly clarify these points.

While the rabbi or counselor has an obligation to protect the student's religious well-being, there is clearly a similar obligation to protect his physical health. A person who has already engage in certain types of homosexual behavior should be considered at serious life-threatening risk for AIDS and needs immediate health counseling. While it may be necessary to say outright that some specific behavior is anti-halakhic, it is also necessary to make clear that counseling is a process that takes time. It is important for the students to be kept safe while the process continues and, although desirable, it is unrealistic simply to demand or expect that non-halakhic behavior cease immediately. The rabbi or counselor has to make this clear, and providing proper health information, including how to protect oneself from disease, is part of this obligation. Similar considerations apply when counseling a promiscuous heterosexual student.

All good religious counseling demands a consideration of compromise during the counseling process, and it makes no difference if the issue is homosexual behavior, masturbation, or *hillul Shabbat*. In our case, presenting total celibacy as the only option might frighten the student into thinking that there is no hope. Therefore, there should be a discussion of compromise, of homosexual behavior that stops short of *mishkav zakhar*. But the chiseling has an obligation to keep the compromising to a minimum, to avoid turning a *bediavad* into a *lehat'hila*. That is why discussions, while sometimes crucial, should not necessarily be undertaken in the initial session.

Whatever the area of religious conflict, there is a need to focus on the possibility of observing all the mitsvot that are in own's power to fulfill. Indeed, one of the hardest messages to get through to a teenager is that the Torah does not require us to be perfect, but to yearn and strive for perfection. Whatever the outcome of one's sexual struggle, everyone is more than his or her sexuality. However anyone might fail, in the end all people will submit themselves not only to God's judgment but also His love.

NOTES

1. Moshe Halevi Spero, *Handbook of Psychotherapy and Jewish Ethics* (New York: Feldheim, 1986): 159.
2. R. Joseph B. Soloveitchik, "A Eulogy for the Talner Rebbe," in *Shiurei Harav* ed. Joseph Epstein, (Hoboken, NJ: Ktav, 1994), 68.
3. R. Joseph B. Soloveitchik, "Catharsis," *Tradition*, 17: no. 2, (Summer 1978).

Chapter Nine

Rabbinic Interventions in Cases of Pathological Guilt

Seymour Hoffman, Ph.D. and
Rabbi Naphtali Bar-Ilan

In her study on orthodox rabbinic attitudes to mental health professionals, Slanger (1996) makes the following points: "It is important for the mental health profession to assume responsibility for initiating contact with the rabbis and engaging in extensive case recruitment efforts"; ". . . it is essential to acknowledge areas of rabbinic expertise and to harmonize closely with the rabbis in a mutually working alliance"; "Therapeutic approaches which may include participation of the rabbis should be considered".

Below are presented five abbreviated case reports describing the collaborative efforts of a rabbi and a clinical psychologist in the treatment of psychiatric patients.

CASE-1

Jonah, a 28 year old bachelor who several years ago became a "baal teshuva" (repentant), has lived in a hostel for discharged psychiatric patients for the last two years. During the past ten years he has been in psychiatric treatment, which included several hospitalizations. His diagnosis is, Schizophrenia, Unspecified Type and Obsessive-Compulsive Disorder, Mixed Obsessional Thoughts and Acts. He is presently receiving psychopharmacological and psychological treatment at a local mental health clinic.

Jonah was described by his therapist as a highly anxious, insecure, dependent, depressed, suspicious, immature, rigid and perseverative individual who was involved in a compulsive manner with issues of religion, dietary laws, cleanliness and food. These preoccupations severely encumbered his daily functioning, both vocationally and socially. His religious obsessional and compulsive preoccupations included excessive concern regarding observing the dietary laws (e.g., dairy and meat products were compromised as a result of their being in close proximity to each other, etc.); concern that he inadvertently deleted several words from his prayer which prompted him to repeat the prayer and excessive concern regarding the cleanliness of his hands and body, especially before partaking of food and praying.

Jonah had approached several local rabbis about his religious questions and concerns who patiently explained to him the halacha in an attempt to reassure and calm him. However, the intricate explanations only prompted more questions and doubts and increased his anxiety. At the request of the patient, the therapist acceded to the patient's wish to discuss his concerns with a rabbi. Before the meeting, the rabbi met with the therapist to discuss the strategic approach to be taken with the patient.

In the three-way meeting, the rabbi, after hearing the patient's questions and concerns for a half-hour, told the patient that because of his difficult emotional situation, he would be granted a special dispensation, and therefore, for him there were no questions and therefore no need for clarifications or explanations. As of today he did not have to worry if the food he eats has been compromised, and need not concern himself whether he skipped some words in his prayers or whether his body was adequately clean before doing a religious ritual. He was told to repeat this "mantra"—"There are no questions and therefore there is no need for answers". He was also informed that this special dispensation was in force for three months and to be renewed only after prior consultation between the rabbi and therapist. The rabbi wrote out his opinion, dated it, and gave it to the therapist to keep. At the conclusion of the session the rabbi wished the patient a speedy recovery and success in his endeavors.

In the following therapy session with the therapist, the patient reported a significant reduction in his religious obsessions. Whenever the patient attempted to raise religious concerns in the session, the therapist reminded him of the "mantra" and the discussion was refocused on other non-religious issues. Several years later, the patient's present therapist reported that the patient continues to use this "mantra" when plagued by religious obsessions, with partial success.

CASE-2

Joseph is a 50 year old haredi (ultra-orthodox) man who three years ago married a divorcee with two children. He has three children from his first marriage whom he sees at rare occasions. For the last ten years he has run a large haredi school in Jerusalem with considerable success.

In the first meeting, he informed the therapist that he is a closed person, doesn't have many friends, doesn't trust people including his wife, and that he will not reveal personal information to the therapist. When asked about his marriage he responded that it was fine, his wife was a good woman and he took all the blame for all the difficulties between them. When pressed, he acknowledged that he feels like a guest in his home, he has no say regarding the discipline of his wife's children and because of his generosity with money (buys presents for his children and their mother), the bank account is in his wife's name. He doesn't have his own pelephone because his wife objects that he speaks to his former wife.

When asked why he decided to go for psychological treatment, he explained that he is not living a meaningful and productive life, lacks desire and energy to cope with life's everyday problems, and feels depressed and pessimistic about the future. When the therapist commented that it was understandable in light of his marital situation, Joseph insisted that he was the blame and that he had to work on himself to accept the situation for the sake of "shalom bayit" (domestic peace). He added that he had to work on his "middot" (attributes), "bitul hayesh" ("annihilation of the self") and learn to accept his situation with grace and tolerance. He denied that he harbored any angry feelings towards his wife and added that angry feelings are prohibited by halacha. Upon inquiry, he acknowledged that angry feelings were unacceptable in his house since he can remember. When asked if he discussed the above mentioned halachic-philosophical issues with a rabbi, he answered in the negative and explained that there wasn't any rabbi that he respected and trusted enough to confide in. At this point, the patient enquired if the therapist would arrange a meeting with a rabbi that the latter respected and trusted in order to discuss these issues.

At the following session (fifth), the rabbi met with Joseph together with the therapist at the latter's office and related to the halachic-philosophical issues raised by the patient. The rabbi opined that the patient's understanding and interpretation of the hassidic concept "bitul hayesh" was inaccurate as it had to be balanced and not create negative consequences. He also took issue regarding the patient's understanding of the halacha's view of anger. According to Rabbi Kook, the rabbi explained, when anger is a mode of life or when it is unjustified, it is prohibited. When a person is wronged, he is permitted to express his natural feelings. At this point the psychologist turned to the rabbi and stated that in his opinion Joseph was hiding behind a "halachic-philosophical smokescreen" in order to avoid acknowledging and dealing with his pent-up angry feelings and fears of behaving in an honest, forthright and assertive manner. He believes that by acting as a "doormat", he is acting in a righteous manner. The rabbi turned to the patient and encouraged him to start taking small steps toward assertiveness and suggested that the next meeting that he schedules with the therapist be done with his new pelephone, even though he may jeopardize "shalom bayit". Joseph unexpectedly responded that if the rabbi rules such, he will do it.

Several days later, Joseph called for an appointment with his new pelephone. At the meeting, Joseph seemed more relaxed and in a positive mood. He reported that he is more assertive at home and was surprised that he met less resistance from his wife than expected. At the end of the session, he mentioned that the previous meeting with the rabbi was very helpful and asked the therapist to again thank the latter for his help.

CASE-3

David, a 29-year-old single man from a religious Iraqi family, is the youngest of six children and the only one who had not completed a high school education. At the age of 19 he was hospitalized with a diagnosis of chronic paranoid schizophrenia. In the past, David had worked in the post office and in sheltered workshops. He is presently involved in a rehabilitation program that involves occupational and social therapy and individual supportive therapy. In one of the therapy sessions, David raised the issue of masturbation. On the one hand he felt extreme conflict and guilt indulging in this behavior: on the other hand, he had no other avenue to release his strong sexual impulses. The guilt caused him considerable distress, depression and preoccupation with thoughts of punishment and suicide. The therapist suggested to David to discuss this issue with a rabbi and after receiving his consent, a meeting was arranged with a rabbi with wide experience in pastoral counseling.

After listening to the patient explain his conflict and dilemma, the rabbi, using appropriate halachic texts, counseled the patient to attempt to control his masturbatory activity since it was against Jewish law. He pointed out, however, that it was not possible to judge him since others could not know what he is feeling and experiencing. Because of his serious psychological problems he could be considered an *anoos (legal term for a person who has limited or no self-control and free choice regarding his behavior)* by society and especially, by his family. The rabbi added that David knew himself best: if he tried to control his behavior and did not succeed, it was an indication that he is an *anoos*. Therefore, there is no reason for guilt feelings. David mentioned to the rabbi that several years ago he had consulted a rabbi about the same issue and was told that his behavior was terrible and sinful, and that if he continued, an accident would befall him. The rabbi pointed out to the patient that since the dire predicted consequences did not occur, it proved that he might be considered an *anoos*. The rabbi terminated the meeting with a quote from the Talmudic text, "Ethics of the Fathers": "You are not called upon to complete the work, yet you are not free to evade it". A week later, the therapist contacted the rabbi and informed him that following the meeting there was a noticeable improvement in the patient's mood and general functioning and thanked him for his help.

CASE-4

Dinah, a thirty year old married woman and mother of three children requested an immediate appointment as she was afraid that out of desperation, she will do harm to herself. The patient appeared tense and anxious as she described her fragile emotional state. For the last two years, after a religious friend of hers in whom she confided, told her that in the Talmud it states that the punishment for not keeping vows is the premature death of children, she has been obsessed with guilt feelings, fears and thoughts of making vows and receiving divine punishment for not fulfilling them. Her emotional stability has been further aggravated as a result of marital tension and conflict.

Following the initial session, Dinah felt less anxious and tense and in more control of her emotions. In the fourth meeting when she again raised the issue of her obsessional thoughts and fears, the therapist suggested a meeting with a religious authority in order to discuss further this issue, to which the patient enthusiastically agreed.

In discussing the case with the rabbi, the therapist suggested that the former arrange a religious ceremony of "Hatarat Nedarim", (Annulment of Vows)[1] as a means of aiding the patient to free herself from the oppressive bonds of her obsessional fears (Rapaport, 1991).

The meeting was held in the rabbi's synagogue and was attended by the therapist and another man. The rabbi, after listening to the patient's story, explained that it is a sin to make vows and not fulfill them but thoughts of making vows are not prohibited.

The Torah, however, realized that man is only human and is not capable of controlling all the time his speech and, therefore, provided a way to annul vows that were made impulsively and now regretted. After explaining the form and purpose of the above mentioned religious ritual, the rabbi conducted the ceremony with the participation of the other two men. At the conclusion of the meeting, the patient, visibly relieved, thanked the rabbi for his help. The latter wrote out what transpired at the meeting, signed the note and asked the other two participants to do likewise and handed it to the patient for future reference.

In the following therapy session, the patient reported a marked decrease in her obsessional thoughts and a significant improvement in her mood and overall functioning.

CASE-5

The patient, a 25 year old bachelor who immigrated to Israel with his mother and older sister five years ago, appeared at the clinic with the following complaints: severe depression, poor concentration, pains in the chest and legs, decreased functioning at work, and an overpowering feeling that he was "going crazy" from his constant thoughts regarding the death of his father. Though he had suffered for the last ten years, he refused to seek psychiatric aid until his mother pleaded with him to do so.

His father, who suffered from several serious physical illnesses and who had a long psychiatric history, expressed a desire to end his life. One day the patient found him attempting to hang himself from a basement rafter. The father asked the son to move the table upon which he was standing so that he could die, but the son refused. After repeated taunting and pleading the son in an attempt to appease his father, moved the table from under his father's feet and immediately returned it to its original place. The father, enraged at his son's action, began cursing and yelling at him to move the table. The son again moved the table, but this time was unsuccessful in returning it to its original place because of the father's frantic kicking movements. The patient immediately ran to his mother for help, but on their return, the father had already expired.

A year before seeking psychiatric help, the patient established a relationship with a woman, with whom he was presently sharing an apartment, but not his "awful secret." The patient felt that he could not marry and bring children into the world because of his fear of not being able to function as a husband and father and "going crazy."

In the therapy sessions, an attempt was made to relate to and deal with the patient's intense and overwhelming guilt feelings regarding the "patricidal" act and his self-punishing behavior, but with little success. At one point, the therapist suggested consulting a rabbi regarding the possibility of atonement for the patient. The patient, who came from a traditional background, agreed. However, he requested that the therapist speak to the rabbi first, in order to prepare him for the "shocking" story. In the meeting with the rabbi, the psychologist presented briefly the patient's history and the purpose and goals of the upcoming meeting.

The meeting with the patient was held in a synagogue in the presence of the psychologist. After hearing the patient's story, the rabbi stated that the offense committed was indeed very serious. He proceeded to explicate on Judaism's view of the sanctity of life and then read several select portions from Maimonides on repentance. The rabbi then concluded:

"According to the Torah, you are obligated to believe that nothing stands in the way of repentance and this includes even the serious offence that you committed. I am also not convinced that all the responsibility falls upon you, in view of your father's erratic condition and disturbed behavior. The Torah requires that the penitent go through a process of experiencing and suffering guilt feelings and regret for the offense committed, a process that you have undergone more than is required and it is a pity that it has continued for so long. You are now required to pass on to the second stage of identity change[2] and doing good and charitable deeds. It seems to me that you can realize identity change by getting married and having children. By naming your child after your deceased father, you will be perpetuating his memory for generations. You should also take upon yourself to donate money to a worthwhile charity in your father's name, visit his grave and in the presence of family members pronounce the new path that you have taken upon yourself and say the Kaddish. God's mercy will never cease and may he provide you with a complete recovery and forgive your sins."

The patient was given the written opinion of the rabbi as he had requested and instructed to take it home to study. He was told it might take him a while to digest the significance of the meeting and the content of the letter and that he should contact the therapist when he felt ready for a meeting. A half-year later, the patient's girlfriend telephoned to invite the therapist to their wedding and requested that he ask the rabbi to officiate as he had offered in his initial meeting with the patient. In response to the therapist's inquiry, she reported that her fiancé was doing well and there was a significant decrease in his somatic complaints. The meeting and letter of the rabbi had a profound influence on him, as it forced him to face reality. She mentioned that several weeks ago, he had visited his father's grave, where he had announced his intention to marry and asked his father for his blessing. A week before the wedding, the couple had a premarital consultation meeting with the rabbi and the following day the patient donated several volumes of religious books, including the writings of Maimonides, to the synagogue, in his father's memory.

CONCLUSION

In the above cases, the rabbis' role and interventions aided the patients to extricate themselves from the guilt-ridden quicksand which imprisoned them.

The result was a considerable remission in their suffering and symptoms and a freeing of their energies and thoughts toward change and growth.

While the psychotherapist can explore the subject of guilt, morality, conscience, etc., he cannot participate with the guilty person in repentance, confession, and atonement or offer dispensations. Here, only that person whom the "guilty" man "acknowledges as a hearer and speaker who represent the transcendence believed in by the "guilty" man", can speak. (Buber, 1965)

In the first case described above, the Orthodox Rabbis through their good intentions, by explaining and analyzing the halachic intricacies of the patient's questions, inadvertently reinforced the patient's obsessive-compulsive behavior, and in the third case, the Orthodox Rabbi, unintentionally, increased the patient's anxiety and guilt feelings and aggravated his unstable mental condition, because of their unfamiliarity and ignorance of psychopathology.

Rabbi Shlomo Wolbe, a prominent haredi rabbi, author and educator from Israel, wrote, "There is an urgent need to organize courses for practicing rabbis and educators, in order to disseminate basic knowledge of the symptoms of neurosis and psychosis and their treatment, in order that they will know to refer mentally ill people immediately to the psychiatrist. Basic knowledge will remove many prejudices". (Wolbe, 1989)

It is strongly recommended that the recommendations of Slanger and Wolbe be adopted by mental health practitioners and clergymen of all faiths, for the benefit of the people they serve.

NOTES

1. It is considered a fearsome sin for one to violate vows and oaths ("He shall not desecrate his word"—Numbers, 30:3) and the mainstream rabbinic view was against making vows in general ("Do not form the habit of making vows"—Babylonian Talmud, Nedarim, 20,a). However, Jewish law provides the possibility of annulment of vows if the vow involves only oneself. One remedy is the ceremony of "Hatarat Nedarim", recited on the eve of Rosh Hashana, the Jewish New Year. In this ceremony, three individuals band together and take turns in constituting a quasi- ecclesiastical court. The petitioner recites a formula whereby he renounces all oaths and promises made and not fulfilled. He expresses regret in taking upon himself vows and requests that they be annulled. The "judges" then declare that there "does not exist any vows" . . . "but there does exist pardon, forgiveness and atonement". The ceremony is concluded with the petitioner declaring for the final time that "he cancels from this time onward all vows and all oaths". The ceremony is declared proactive so that if an oath is made subsequently and then regretted, it too is declared totally null and void.

2. Part of the therapeutic process in cases of Post-Traumatic Stress Disorder of "accident killers" is "to forgive themselves and move on to **redefinition and acceptance of the self**". See, Janoff-Bulman, Shattered Assumptions: Towards a New Psychology of Trauma, 1992, New York: The Free Press.

REFERENCES

M Buber, "Guilt and guilt feelings", in *The Knowledge of Man,* ed. M Friedman (New York: Harper Torchbooks, 1965).

JL Rapaport, *The Boy Who Couldn't Stop Washing.* (New York: Signet, 1991), 176–191.

C Slanger, "Orthodox rabbinic attitudes to mental health professionals and referral patterns." *Tradition* 31, no. 1 (1996) 22–33.

S Wolbe, "Psychiatry and religion," in *In the Pathways of Medicine*, 5, (1989), (Hebrew).

Chapter Ten
Psychotherapy and Honoring Parents
Seymour Hoffman, Ph.D.

Rabbi Yitzchok Zilberstein, a respected halachic authority from Bnei Brak, Israel, was presented with the following brief case study preceded by a short introduction, in reaction to his halachic decision published in "Assia" many years ago (5747).

A considerable number of difficulties, problems and psychopathology of children (and adults who are stuck in their childhood) are a result of parental "misbehavior" (double messages, exploitations, excessive demands, criticism and expectations, involvement of his child in parental conflicts, engenderment of excessive guilt feelings, etc.).

In psychological treatment the therapist attempts to aid the child (adult) to understand, recognize and identify his inner conflicts, fears, anxieties, ambivalent feelings and the troublesome and pathological behavior that stems from them and help him develop more effective and appropriate ways to cope with his internal conflicts and life's stresses and demands.

In individual, family and group therapy, the therapist at times may encourage the patient, directly or indirectly, to externalize and express his pent up angry feelings toward the significant people in his life—his boss, spouse, sibling or parent, rather than suppress and internalize them, since this can result in the development of somatic symptoms, excessive guilt and self punishment and a distorted negative self image.

Question: Are the above therapeutic interventions permissible since this may cause the patient to transgress "Cursed be he that dishonors his father and mother".

To explicate the question, a brief case study is presented:

An 18-year-old university coed applied to the counseling service because of severe depression, intense social anxiety and difficulty in concentration in her studies. This was done without her parent's knowledge for fear that they would punish her.

In the third session, the patient, with great hesitancy and anguish, revealed to her therapist that, from the age of ten, her father has been sexually abusing her. Against her will, he had touched the intimate parts of her body, kissed her on the lips and insisted that the door to her bedroom be ajar and the door of the shower room unlocked when she bathed.

The patient slept uneasily at night and showered while wearing her undergarments for fear of an expected visit from her father. The patient did not *protest* for fear of being totally rejected and/or punished by her father. She did not tell her mother because the latter was weak and always sided with her husband. The patient felt that she was in some way responsible for her father's behavior and attempted to diminish her "femininity" by losing a great deal of weight, thus endangering her health. She viewed herself as a wicked person who deserved punishment and frequently inflicted upon herself bodily harm in order to "atone for her sins." She had frequently entertained suicidal thoughts but never attempted to end her life.

The goals of therapy were to help the patient view herself as a victim and not as a partner to sinful behavior, to give legitimacy to her pent-up anger toward her father, encourage her to externalize rather than internalize her feelings and stand up and repudiate her father's inappropriate, non-paternal behavior.

Gradually, the patient became more assertive and repelled her father's advances and insisted that her bedroom door be closed and the shower room door be locked when she bathed. In the therapy sessions, she permitted herself to speak more freely about her fear and hatred of her father and her anger and disappointment in her mother. The patient started to gain weight, dress in an appropriate feminine fashion and increase her social contacts. Her self-image improved as well as her concentration and academic work. A year after termination of therapy, the patient married and graduated from the university with high marks.

From a halachic perspective did the therapist fulfill the following commandments?

1) "Cause him to be thoroughly healed" (Exodus, 21, 19);

2) "Return it to him" (Exodus, 23, 4); i.e., mental health: and "Neither shall thou stand idly by the blood of thy neighbor" (Leviticus, 19, 16), for one can view the father, in this case, as a pursuer" who is endangering the mental health and well being of his daughter, or did he unwittingly cause the patient to transgress "Cursed be he that dishonors his father and mother"?

Rabbi Zilberstein's response:

One has to divide the answer into two parts:

1) In a situation where the father has not repented and continues in his wicked ways.

2) Where the father has repented.

Regarding the first situation, it is stated in the Shulchan Aruch (standard book of Jewish law), Yoreh Deah, chapter 240, paragraph 18 in the glosses or the Rama, "Some say that as long as the father did not repent, there is no obligation to honor him."

In light of this opinion, there is no question since there is no obligation to honor a wicked father. However, this is not so simple since the Schach comments there (ibid, subparagraph 20), "Even though there is no obligation to honor him, it is prohibited to distress him". Note it.

In light of this, if the father discovers that his daughter is receiving psychological treatment and is being encouraged and directed to vent her negative feelings toward him, he will be distressed, and this is prohibited.

It could be that even if the father does find out that his daughter is receiving psychological treatment, it is permissible, for the prohibition to demean and disrespect him is only when the aim is for the sake of denigration but not when it is done for therapeutic purposes and for the benefit of his daughter which in the end is for his benefit also, so that he will have a healthy daughter, suitable for marriage and the continuation of his progeny and this is not "embarrassment" but "rehabilitation" and preparation for marriage. And proof that it is permitted to shame and distress the father for desirable benefits is derived from King Hezekiah who dragged his father's bones on a bed of sackcloth as is explained in the tractate Pesachim, 56. Rashi explained there that he dragged his father's bones for his atonement and did not bury him in kingly splendor, for the sanctification of God, that he be censured for his wickedness and his wicked deeds be removed.

The tractate concludes that the sages acknowledged that he acted correctly. Therefore, it is permitted to humiliate a father for a benefit and especially when the father destroyed his daughter's world, he is obligated to suffer in order that she be cured.

And if the father repented, one can assume that he prefers that his daughter despise him in her heart in order that she can marry and that this will be his atonement for what he did to her and maybe it is proper to involve and consult the father regarding the therapeutic process in order to prevent as much as possible his embarrassment.

And after the daughter is cured and her wounds are healed, it is proper to urge her to return to respect her father for she is obligated to him for bringing her into the world and in spite of the damage that he inflicted on her, her debt to her father has not expired.

In summary, the above treatment is permissible and the psychologist fulfilled the aforementioned commandments.

Psychologist comments:

It appears that the rabbi's lenient ruling applies only to parents who are viewed halachically as "wicked" and therefore their permission for their children to receive psychological treatment (where they are free to express their negative feelings toward their "wicked" parents) is not required. It is not clear whether children (youngster and adults) of "non-wicked" parents are permitted to receive psychological treatment against the wishes of their parents (who unintentionally have and are presently causing psychological problems and emotional difficulties to their children—see introductory remarks) who either deny that their children have emotional and behavioral problems, don't believe in psychological treatment or are embarrassed that other people know of their problems and conflicts.

Is the prohibition, "Cursed be he that dishonors his father and mother" inapplicable to treatment situations where the goals are healing and rehabilitation, or does the honor of parents take precedence over the aforementioned goals?

The above question has relevance not only to the religious therapist but also to the religious patient who may be hesitant and reluctant to discuss his problems, conflicts and feelings openly for fear of transgressing a biblical prohibition.

Rabbi Zilberstein's response:

If the father is not "wicked," one is not permitted to go against his wishes regarding his declination of psychological treatment (for his child), unless by rabbinic decree. And if this is brought before a rabbi and he is of the opinion that it is in the best interest of the child to receive psychological treatment, the father has no authority to dispute with the rabbi. The judgment of a rabbi is similar to that of a court and it is a commandment to listen to the words of the sages. If the father does not fulfill his commandment, there is no obligation to honor him. Even if the rabbi instructs the father to permit his child to speak about him, this is not disparagement but a form of healing. Furthermore, the father also bears some guilt in that he caused this situation. Therefore, there is no slighting of his honor, rather healing and rehabilitation of the child.

Comments by Rabbi Naftali Bar-Ilan, Community Rabbi of Rehovot, Israel.

Regarding the article on "Psychotherapy and Honoring Parents", the most important lesson we can learn from this article is that one should not present general questions to a rabbi (and that the rabbi should not respond to general questions) but provide specific, relevant and pertinent information so that the rabbi can direct his response to the specific person and situation.

Secondly, Rabbi Zilberstein is of the opinion that there are situations that one should turn to a mental health expert for help and that psychological treatment can be permissible according to halacha, even if it involves offending the honor of parents. However, one should be careful not to offend the honor of parents when it is not vital to the treatment. Therefore, this kind of treatment is permissible only when it is vital to treatment, there is the possibility that it will succeed, and that the offending behavior towards the parents will not exceed that which is required for the treatment to succeed.

The halachic ruling regarding psychological treatment is similar to halachic rulings regarding medical treatments that involve halachic prohibitions. For example, in a situation where an abortion is being contemplated, the physician should provide the pertinent information to a rabbi and he will decide according to halacha, whether to permit performing the abortion.

Chapter Eleven

Halacha and Psychological Treatment Dilemmas and Conflicts

Seymour Hoffman, Ph.D.

Religion (halacha) and Mental Health (Psychotherapy) share a common concern and goal—the quality of life and its improvement and enrichment. Religion provides man with a purpose, direction, ethical and moral rules and values to make his life more meaningful and worthwhile. Psychotherapy's purpose and function is first, to give the troubled person relief from suffering, to ease his psychic pain, and then to equip him better to live in peace, affection and stable equilibrium with himself, his immediate objects and the world around him.

However, there are basic differences between the two disciplines. While psychotherapy is anthropocentric, religion is theocentric. While the former's goal and measuring rod is man's psychological well-being (however defined by the mental health expert), the latter's goal and measuring rod is man's ethical behavior and obedience to the will of God. Halacha does not recognize man's rights but the duties of man to God.

Religious values therefore, may at times differ and be incongruent with the values held by mental health professionals.

Behavior that may by unacceptable from a religious standpoint, may be acceptable, if not preferable, from a mental health perspective (e.g. masturbation as occasional outlet for sexual impulses; abortion for a woman emotionally unsuitable, incapable or unprepared for the demands of a mothering role, etc.)

In the practice of psychotherapy, the religious therapist will at times be faced with conflicts between his religious and mental health values and goals.

Two issues that frequently present halachic dilemmas are psychotherapy and honoring parents and confidentiality and religious obligations. Several examples are presented below.

Rabbi Yitzchok Zilberstein, a respected halachic authority, was asked the following question by a psychologist: "If during a psychological evaluation, the psychologist forms the opinion that the child's problems are related to the detrimental relationship with his parents because of his and/or their problems, is it permissible for the psychologist to bring this to the child's attention?" The rabbi's response (which appeared in "Assia," 2-43, 11,2-3, Nison, 5747) was:

"It is prohibited to make the child aware of the contribution of his parents to his problems lest he cause him to transgress, 'Cursed be he that dishonors his father and mother' (Deuteronomy, 26, 16) and one does not cure through transgressions."

Rabbi Eliezer Melamed, Rosh Yeshiva, Beth-El, commented in the weekly "Arutz-7 (27. 1. 05), in his article , "Psychologists and Honoring Parents": "Problem of Psychologists":

Many psychologists nowadays tend to blame a patient's problems on his parents;[1] they pressured him, got angry at him, and even hit him. In other words, "abused" him. Since the patient is considered a victim of his parent's treatment, it follows that he himself is never to blame for his troubles. His conscience can be clear and he can free himself from his distress. The parents are to blame for all his problems and troubles which he inflicts upon himself and his surroundings.

From this perspective, it is clear that the relationship between the child and parents will worsen and with the encouragement of the psychologist, he will scornfully transgress the commandment of honoring parents.

Even if such a treatment would have been psychologically effective, it is nevertheless forbidden to take part in it since it is against the laws of the Torah.

Just as a person is not allowed to steal or murder in order to relieve himself of suffering, so he may not transgress the commandment of respecting his parents in order to relieve himself of suffering.

Rabbi Nachum Rabinovitch, Rosh Yeshiva, Birkat Moshe, Maaleh Adumim was presented with the following question.

A middle-aged religious mother of five children mentioned in the initial therapy session that her husband was physically abusive to her and her children, as was her father toward her and her mother. "My father was a terrible person. Am I allowed to say that?"

What is the halachic position regarding children (young or adult) speaking disparagingly and expressing anger and hate toward their parents in the therapy session (individual, family, group)? Is it permissible since the purpose and goal are healing and rehabilitation of the tormented and dysfunctional patient, or prohibited because of the biblical injunction, "Cursed be he that dishonors his father and mother"?

The above question has relevance not only to the religious therapist but also to the religious patient who may be hesitant to discuss his problems, conflicts and feelings openly for fear of transgressing a biblical prohibition.

Rabbi Rabinovitch's response:

In reply to your letter of 21/5, the halacha is very clear on this point. See *psachim* 56a where it is related about מלך חזקיהו: "גירר עצמות אביו על מיטה של חבלים", and the sages praised him for this. See also Rashi's explanation on the spot, that his intent was to bring atonement for his father by causing others to repent. If it is done for a constructive goal and in an effective manner, the prospects are that speaking about the sins of the fathers will help bring them atonement. Nonetheless, even if the father was wicked one most not curse him. This has nothing to do with bringing into the open disgust and revulsion towards his transgressions.

Psychologist's comment:

Your permissive ruling seems restricted to "wicked" parents who benefit (receive atonement) as a result of the "negative" behavior (expression of anger, resentment, hate) toward them, in the treatment session.

Since most parents would not be considered "wicked" even though they may have caused, unwittingly, emotional turmoil and damage to their offsprings, to a greater or lesser extent (through preferential treatment, conflicting and double messages, exploitation, engenderment of excessive guilt feeling, unrealistic expectations and demands, etc.) which may result in expressed, repressed and suppressed anger and resentment on the part of the child towards them, may the therapist facilitate these pent-up negative feelings to become more accessible to the child's awareness? May he encourage the child to speak freely about his negative feelings toward his parents, if in the therapists view, this is necessary for the therapy to succeed? In a nutshell, can a child (young, adult) "bad-mouth" his parents (even though they aren't considered "wicked" and are against psychological treatment), if the purpose and goal is not to degrade the parents but to free the child from his debilitating symptoms and enable him to function more effectively?

Rabbi Rabinovitch's response:

In my previous reply I cited an example of a wicked parent as an extreme case. Whenever a wrong is committed there is an element of wickedness, even if unintentional, which requires atonement. Obviously one's attitude to any person, including his parents, must take into account the good elements as well as the bad ones. Negative feelings, too, have to be integrated into a total perspective. If the expression of negative feelings is intended to bring about a therapeutic result, it is certainly justified.

On the other hand, one must always bear in mind that real or imaginary hurts are sometimes exaggerated far out of proportion. It would seem to me that part of the therapist's task is to help the patient see things in their proper perspective, and thus to enable pent-up feeling to be released in a controlled manner. Even a child needs to learn to see the total picture, even when it is necessary to "bad mouth" certain aspects of it.

The second question posed to Rabbi Rabinovitch dealt with the sensitive and complex issue of professional confidentiality and one's religious obligations.

A woman confided to her psychologist in a treatment session that she had not been attending the mikvah (ritualarium) for the last several months and doesn't plan to in the future, without the knowledge of her husband.

Is the therapist obligated to betray professional confidence and inform her husband that his wife is causing him to transgress a biblical prohibition? Does the biblical prohibition, "Thou shall not stand idly by the blood of thy neighbor" (Leviticus, 19,16), apply in this situation?

On the other hand, betraying professional confidence will possibly 1) cause the client to discontinue vital psychological treatment; 2) discourage other people that are in need of psychological treatment from going to religious psychotherapists; 3) significantly reduce potential referrals, and thereby, the therapist's income.[2]

Rabbi Rabinovitch's response:

I wonder whether a patient's statement to her therapist is necessarily credible. Even if there were no doubt at all about its truth, it still would not have the status of certain knowledge for the therapist, and especially in view of the fact that patients are known to invent tales in fulfillment of desires of one kind or another.

In any case, it seems to me that a religious therapist is duty-bound to find ways to try to convince his patient not to transgress. I realize that some psychologists are opposed to a judgmental stance, but such opposition seems to me to be against Torah law.

Psychologist's comment:
Your response seems to relate to the issue of "judgmental stance" of therapists rather than to the question posed.

Regarding the issue raised, my humble opinion is that a psychotherapist is obligated and has an unwritten contract with his client, to help him cope more effectively with problems, conflicts and issues that are of concern to him and which are causing him distress and difficulty in his everyday functioning (and not issues that are of concern to the religious practitioner, even though I accept the argument that man's contract with God supersedes man's contract with man). Furthermore, raising (no matter how sensitively) religious and moral issues (mikvah, abortion, etc.) which are non-issues and of no concern to the non-committed client, will all probability, cause him to flee from vital psychological treatment, as he will interpret the therapist's behavior as "missionary" and not therapeutic.[3]

Rabbi Rabinovitch's response:
Your most recent letter is quite puzzling to me. You describe the psychologist's task admirably. However, may I be permitted to raise a trivial question. Consider the case of a patient who has decided to murder his aged grandmother in order to acquire her wealth. This decision causes him no end of problems and conflicts, as well as "distress, anxiety and malfunctioning in his daily life," to the point that he finds himself not only unable to go through with his plan effectively, but is also hampered in other areas. Is the therapist obligated or even permitted to help the patient cope in a manner that will lead to the effective and successful fulfillment of his plan and make him a wealthy person?

To ask about the prohibition of לא תעמוד, it seems to me, is to accept the fundamental premise that a therapist too owes his first obligation to הקב"ה and there can be no escape into a value-neutral so-called "professional" world. From a religious point of view, genuine mental health can only be attained on the basis of sound morality. A cheat and a fraud who is totally undisturbed by his actions is not a healthy specimen.

In conclusion, I thought that my previous letter contained an answer to your question, conditional upon the therapist's evaluation of the truth value of the patient's statement. Even if the therapist feels that the patient's stated intention to mislead and entrap her husband is only a fantasy, it would seem to me that there is a duty to try to guide the patient to a healthy recognition that such fantasies are not to be realized in practice.[4]

NOTES

1. Jewish sources are also "guilty" of this. See Kings-1, 1, 6.

Rabbi Samson Raphael Hirsch in his commentary on the verse, "When the boys grew up. . ." (Genesis, 25, 27), states, "They (Sages) point out that the striking contrast in the grandchildren of Abraham may have been due, not so much to a difference in their temperaments as to mistakes in the way they were brought up". "The great principle, 'Bring up each child in accordance with its own way', was forgotten".

Rabbi Yaacov Kanievsky ("Orchot Yosher", p. 34) makes the point "that if father and mother are not identical in their speech; one says right and one says left, and the son sees quarrels, then he is not executed as a "stubborn and rebellious" son, since his parents are at fault and not him".

2. One can add to the above concerns: 1) The therapist's reputation and position may be detrimentally affected; 2) He may be liable to suits; 3) He will be transgressing the state's/country's laws and may be liable to punishment (including imprisonment).

3. "Reprove not a scorner, lest he hate thee". (Proverbs, 9, 8). "A scorner does not love to be reproved. He will not go unto the wise". (Proverbs, 15, 12)

"Rabbi Elaah in the name of Rabbi Elazar, the son of Rabbi Shimon said: 'Just as it is a commandment upon man to say what will be heard, so it is a commandment upon man not to say what will not be heard'". (Yevamot, 65, 2) Rashi adds: "It is written: 'Thou shall surely rebuke thy neighbor'—rebuke who that receives from you."

4. Another prominent rabbi and recognized posek (arbiter) from Bnei Brak, when presented with this dilemma, responded directly to the above question: "It is clear that the therapist is obligated to inform the husband" and used a similar example cited by Rabbi Rabinovitch to make his point.

Rabbi, Dr., Mordechai Halperin's response to above question was: "That under the above circumstances, the answer is negative". (Personal communication).

Rabbi Alfred Cohen presented his views regarding betraying professional confidences, in his article on "Privacy: A Jewish Perspective", which appeared in the Journal of Halacha and Contemporary Society (82, 1981).

"A person whose livelihood depends upon maintaining the confidentiality of revelations made to him, need not jeopardize his position by telling those secrets. Although keeping silent might violate the negative mitzvah (commandment) of not standing by and allowing another Jew to be harmed, yet as long as he is not violating the mitzvah by *doing* any action, and were he to act would endanger his own livelihood, then he is permitted to remain silent. . .

"Even if there would be no monetary loss involved for the counselor, yet there remains the question whether professional counseling could continue as a viable activity if the public could not rely upon absolute inviolability of confidence. . .

"Obviously, fear of exposure would preclude many persons from seeking help they desperately need. . .*

"Is it beneficial for the community to have available to it people with skill and knowledge to help those in pain and confusion? I think yes, very much so. Can we allow this benefit to the community to take precedence over the rights and prerogatives of the individuals within the community? The preponderance of rabbinical opinion in this area leads clearly to the conclusion that the public needs override the personal welfare of the individual."

See M. H. Spero's comment to Rabbi Cohen's article, ("Halachic definitions of confidentiality in the psychotherapeutic encounter: Theory and practice"), in Tradition, 1982, 20, 4, 298-326.

---

*Rabbi Naphtali Bar-Ilan, Community Rabbi, Rehovot, Israel, was asked the following question:

Is a psychotherapist, upon discovering that his patient is committing a serious transgression against the Torah, obligated to rebuke him/her because of the positive commandment, "Thou shall certainly rebuke thy neighbor and not suffer sin on his account" (Leviticus, 19:17).

Rabbi Bar-Ilan's response:

1. Psychotherapists are obligated to observe the commandment of "rebuke".
2. The obligation of "rebuke" exists only when there is a possibility that the words will be heard and considered seriously.
3. The obligation of "rebuke" exists only if there is no chance that it will cause physical or mental/emotional damage to the patient. That is also the reason why there is no obligation when there is a chance that as a result of the "rebuke", the patient will discontinue his treatment.
4. There is no obligation of "rebuke" if the therapist is afraid that damage may be caused to his reputation or that the patient may complain to the authorities or sue him.
5. There is no obligation of "rebuke" if it may cause people to lose their trust in religious therapists and therefore, fewer people who need psychological treatment, will turn to them for help. In view of the above reservations, it seems that the chance that the therapist will be obligated to fulfill the commandment of "rebuke" is quite limited.

However, the religious therapist should carefully evaluate and discern throughout the treatment process and afterwards, if the opportunity does present itself without producing negative consequences.

Rabbi Shabtai Rappoport, Rosh Yeshiva, "Shevut Yisroel", was asked the following question:

Is a therapist obligated to terminate marital therapy with a couple upon discovering that the husband is a kohen and the wife is a divorcee ("mesayeah lidvar aveira"-aiding in the commission of a transgression)?

Rabbi Rappoport's response:

The question you raise should be examined from two aspects—the obligation of a non professional person in these circumstances, and the differences, if any, between a non professional and a professional.

A non professional is obliged by the mitzvah of "tochecha" (rebuke) to convince a kohen to divorce his forbidden wife. In case it proves impossible, one must not show support to such a couple. Showing such support is a transgression against the prohibition of being a "mesayeah lidvar aveira" as explained by Rav Moshe Feinstein zt"l (Igrot Moshe, Vol. V, Orach Chaim, part 5, Siman 13, paragraph 7). Such indulgence makes the person a sort of an accessory, as all members of the Jewish public should abhor, and show their abhorrence, of transgressing any command.

Here a professional differs. In my opinion he is bound to the mitzva of "tochecha" where relevant. He should endeavor to show the couple that marriage against our Torah could not come to a good end—as he should firmly and honestly believe.

However, when "tochecha" is not possible, his relationship with the couple is not social, and hence he does not relate to them as a member of the Jewish community. In the professional context accepting a situation as a given baseline does not constitute a personal opinion, and thus does not seem as if the professional condones the patient's behavior. A professional who treats a child abuser does not express his opinion regarding this abuse. That is why he is not considered a "mesayeah". (Igrot Moshe ibid).